NINETY-NINE IRON

by

WENDELL GIVENS

with

Arthur Ben and Elizabeth N. Chitty

Seacoast Publishing, Inc.

Birmingham, AL

1992

Published by
SEACOAST PUBLISHING, INC.
P.O. Box 26492
Birmingham, Alabama 35226

Printed in the United States of America

1st printing, 1992

ISBN 1-878561-09-X

Jacket design and book design by Ray Brown

For

Mary Anne Boswell Givens, who enriches lives, especially the author's, and our very special threesome: **Lynn Ray, Becky Freeman** and **Drew Willis**, and their families.

My brother **Vernon Givens**, who made possible my college and newspaper years.

My other brothers and sisters, each of whom has succeeded in a distinctive way:

Leo Givens, Allen Givens, Elaine Gower and **Marjorie Lovell.**

Sewanee's 1899 season

Oct. 21 at Atlanta: Sewanee 12, Georgia 0
Oct. 23 at Atlanta: Sewanee 32, Georgia Tech 0
Oct. 28 at Sewanee: Sewanee 46, Tennessee 0
Nov. 3 at Sewanee: Sewanee 54, Southwestern 0

Nov. 9 at Austin: Sewanee 12, Texas 0
Nov. 10 at Houston: Sewanee 10, Texas A&M
Nov. 11 at New Orleans: Sewanee 23, Tulane
Nov. 13 at Baton Rouge: Sewanee 34, LSU 0
Nov. 14 at Memphis: Sewanee 12, Ole Miss 0

Nov. 20 at Sewanee: Sewanee 71, Cumberland 0
Nov. 30 at Montgomery: Sewanee 11, Auburn 10
Dec. 2 at Atlanta: Sewanee 5, North Carolina 0

12-0-0
Sewanee 322, Opponents 10

Contents

Introduction

Getting to know Sewanee

Answers were needed before this exploration could begin.

Why write the story of a football team that played almost a century ago?

Is sufficient material available?

Does reader potential justify the effort?

My answer to the first question was another: How could a team's feat of winning five games in six days have been so long overlooked for full recounting? Yes, it was pioneer-days football, but the style of play was not all that different from today's. And Sewanee's Iron Men trip has never been matched, not even challenged.

As for available material, surely the university had records — student newspapers, yearbooks, photographs and clippings. Newspapers of that day already were devoting considerable space to football. And wouldn't children and grandchildren of the 1899 players have clippings and photographs, along with memories? For a retired newspaperman who had the opportunity to visit the cities where the Iron Men played and a yen to delve into century-old newspaper files, the prospects were inviting.

Ah, yes, a colleague agreed, it all looks so rosy, but now you have to answer the only question that really matters: Will enough potential readers be interested to make the effort worthwhile? I thought of the oft-quoted mountain climber who climbed "because the mountain was there." I decided to write the story of Sewanee's Iron Men because the story was there, had been there for almost 100 years and had not been recorded in detail.

Thus, I began.

To my 1930s sandlot football team in Montgomery, Ala., Sewanee was just another name in the Sunday football scores and very often a loser. We saw the Tigers play one game and that because the opponent was Alabama and because a friendly policeman looked the other way while we clambered over the wall at Cramton Bowl.

The game was a mismatch as were too many of Sewanee's Southeastern Conference contests. School administrators apparently had had their heads in past glory when they agreed to be an SEC charter member in 1933 and compete against the likes of Alabama, Auburn, Tennessee, Louisiana State and Mississippi. Sewanee dropped out of the conference in 1940.

A few years later I encountered Sewanee again, this time because *Birmingham Age-Herald* sports editor Bob Phillips was a Sewanee alumnus and because I was fortunate enough to join his sports department staff in 1941. Sewanee's football decline had not diminished Phillips' love for and pride in the university.

From Phillips and assistant sports editor Benny Marshall I learned for the first time of the 1899 Sewanee team that had won five games in six days, but by then 1899 seemed ancient history and our football files carried little more than the bare scores from that Sewanee season.

Then in 1952, after having transferred from the sports department to the *Birmingham News* copy desk, I became much better acquainted with Sewanee. As moonlighting editor of a Junior Chamber of Commerce publication that ran brief features on Birmingham people, I decided to do an article on the '99 Sewanee team, focusing on any Birmingham-area players. Bob Phillips knew of my plans and asked, "Would you like to meet the captain of that team?"

"He's still alive? And he's available?"

Henry Goldthwaite Seibels indeed was alive and his insurance company office was only two blocks away!

Phillips made a phone call and told me, "He'll see you at 2 tomorrow afternoon, but don't plan on staying too long. You'll find out why after you get there."

My interest in Sewanee began to jell that day.

Seibels, partner in Jemison-Seibels, was a quiet, friendly

man who knew how to handle a newsman who hadn't done his homework for the interview but who wanted to know all about the Iron Men team. From a stack of mimeographed papers Seibels handed me a copy, wished me well and said politely that he had insurance matters that needed his attention.

Fine with me, I thought. I had enough information, even if canned, for the Junior Chamber publication. I thanked him and departed, and walked away from a gold mine of firsthand information about the '99 Sewanee team.

Decades later, Seibels' two sons, Henry G. Jr. ("Buzz") and Kelly would tell me that their father seldom talked to them about football. "You shouldn't live on past glory," he told them. But many times in recent months, as I put spool after spool of newspaper microfilm on screens, I bemoaned the missed opportunity to have heard the team captain describe the Sewanee Iron Men and their 1899 season.

From time to time in the near-century since Sewanee made its marathon trip, sports columnists have, on slow days, reached for their Sewanee file and retold the Iron Men story. Bob Phillips and longtime *Birmingham News* sports editor Zipp Newman knew Diddy Seibels and a few other surviving members of '99 Sewanee and reminisced with them. Later, Alf Van Hoose and Clyde Bolton of the *News* joined the occasional retelling. Veteran *Nashville Banner* sports editor (in recent years *Banner* executive) Fred Russell probably was best acquainted with Sewanee football, partly because he attended just-down-the-road Vanderbilt, which in the 1890s and early 1900s was a fierce rival of Sewanee.

Anyway, with each retelling of the Sewanee story, I grew more curious as to why apparently no one had researched the Iron Men season and written an in-depth article or a book about it. As a chapter in *Ninety-Nine Iron* relates, the story was told in bits and pieces in newspapers, football histories and ultimately in *Sports Illustrated* magazine in its Oct. 16, 1961, issue.

But virtually all the accounts were barebones and not always totally accurate, so after retiring from the *News* in 1986 I began exploring the possibility of writing an expanded account of the Iron Men season, focusing on the five games in six days. I found stories in daily and college newspapers and in yearbooks, especially at Sewanee. With the generous assistance of people at the University of the South, especially archivist Anne Armour and historiographer Arthur Ben and Elizabeth N. Chitty, I gradually pieced together what I feel is a reasonably accurate account of the 12-game season.

"Reasonably accurate" would not suffice in most research, and I certainly am not happy having to thus qualify in this account. Had I anticipated, when I sat across from Diddy Seibels, that one day I would be researching the Iron Men story in full, fewer "presumablies" and "probablies" would appear in this account.

A similar near-miss occurred decades later in Montgomery where I was attending the 50th-year reunion of my high school class of 1940. Among my Sidney Lanier classmates was a descendant of Seibels on his mother's side. Answering my question about possible clippings or letters he might have, Alfred Goldthwaite remarked that a family member had asked at one point if anyone wished to have a box of Seibels memorabilia and, hearing no positive reply, tossed it onto a trash fire.

The "sports writers" whose play-by-play accounts of Sewanee games are reprinted in this account in all likelihood were police, courthouse and general assignment reporters turned sports writers for a day. Their accounts don't always jibe with accounts in other papers, such as the *Sewanee Purple*, and sometimes they left gaps—such as explanation of crucial officiating calls that often decided the outcome of games - and frequent switching back and forth between present and past tense. But remembering the challenges they faced— covering a still-new sport with an evolving jargon and scrambling between crowded stands and sidelines to get their information—one must give them considerable credit, not criticism. Without those hardy pioneers, the story of the Sewanee Iron Men would be sparse indeed.

In attempting to put meat on the skeleton accounts of '99 Sewanee, I have used newspaper reports, daily and college, on all the "Texas trip" games, plus the Sewanee-Auburn and Sewanee-North Carolina games.

Except for occasional punctuation needs and correction of obvious misspellings, the accounts are verbatim, although, as noted, some leave questions: Play-by-play reports often indicate that although insufficient yardage was made for first downs, a team retained possession; in other instances a team appeared to be driving the ball well, but for some reason elected to punt. Frequent kicks on first or second down were not surprising; a team that had a good punter used his kicks both to keep an opponent backed up and also to avoid losing the ball through fumbling deep in its own territory.

Some of the questions I sought to answer as I dug into the Iron Men story were these:

—How many players actually made the trip west? Various accounts had mentioned as few as 14 and as many as 21. The *Sewanee Purple* settled that once and for all with a rollcall of the 21 men when the squad returned from the five-games-in-six-days trip.

—Who *were* the Iron Men? Most accounts that I had read mentioned only three or four players by name. With assistance of people at the university I found some information on each of the 21 players, plus the coach, manager and trainer. In a few cases the so-called thumbnail sketches are that, no more.

—Perhaps the most intriguing question was: Why in heaven's name would a school schedule five road games, against name institutions, to be played in six days? That question is answered, although not as fully or with as much certainty as it deserves.

—Almost as intriguing: *Who* arranged the schedule? Confessions being good for a researcher's soul—much of this answer is presumed, but circumstantial evidence strongly supports the presumptions.

—What was 1899 football like? From a variety of sources, including two magazines of that day—*Outing* and *Harper's Weekly*—plus rules in effect then, provided by the National Collegiate Athletic Association, a brief description of the game as it was played then became possible.

—What place does Sewanee's marathon feat merit in football history? The question was asked of one of today's top coaches and of an All-American (1930) who played both ways, offense and defense, and was on the field virtually every minute of every game. Their comments, along with some thoughts of my own, appear in the final chapter.

—Last, but certainly not least, I wondered what student life and thought were like at Sewanee when the Iron Men were there. From the 1900 Sewanee yearbook, the *Cap and Gown*; from articles in the campus *Purple*; from three or four books written about the university, and from alumni, a limited description of 1899 campus life was put together. It follows, as a prelude to the story of the Iron Men.

Mood music, please

In his warm, upbeat memoir, *The Better Parts of A Life*, former Sewanee dean and political science professor Robert S. "Red" Lancaster said of his early years at the university: "This was a remarkable time in the history of Sewanee. The old lingered; memories of the beginnings still persisted. The honored dead were still remembered in the homes of the living."

That being true in the 1930s, flip the calendar back to 1899, the year of the football Iron Men, and such memories surely would have been sharper because the times almost touched the beginnings.

Sewanee 1899 was 34 years after the Civil War. The South was still trying to pull itself back together after the ravages of war and Reconstruction. The loss of so many young men from families at all levels of society was a wound that would be long in healing. Reunions of Confederate soldiers were painful reminders of the scarring.

Yet here was the young University of the South, its own 1868 opening delayed by the war, solidly established as a center of learning and already producing leaders for the rebuilding South and for the nation; leaders such as Dr. William Crawford Gorgas, an 1875 graduate and Medical Corps major in the just-ended Spanish-American War. Gorgas soon would become known as the conqueror of yellow fever and, as such, the man who helped make possible the completion of the Panama Canal.

What was Sewanee like during the years of the Iron Men? A few paragraphs further along, an essay from the 1900 *Cap and Gown* will get down to specifics; in advance of that, a capsule look at 1899 is possible thanks to information provided by Sewanee historiographer Arthur Ben and Elizabeth N. Chitty.

Student enrollment in '99 has been mentioned as low as 150, as high as 500. Registration records show it was 326, comprised of 122 students in the college, 26 in theology, 17 in law and 161 in medicine.

The year the Iron Men won an everlasting place in football history for the university, the school's dormitories had no central heat, only fireplaces; no indoor plumbing except for the "running water" that gravity made possible; virtually no telephone service, and only rare sights of the newfangled vehicles called automobiles.

Some faculty members managed to string phone lines from their homes to campus offices. Students wishing to communicate quickly with the home folks could go to the telegraph office and accomplish that. That same telegraph office made possible placing an order to a nearby town for a keg of whiskey, and the keg could be delivered on campus within two or three hours for, say, toasting football victories! School officials did not frown on such toasting, only on over-toasting.

Pomp and circumstance were part of the scene when occasion indicated. So were gowned upperclassmen, appropriately attired (coat and tie) underclassmen, and compulsory chapel attendance.

But even on its hideaway mountaintop and without coeds (they wouldn't arrive until 1969), 1899 Sewanee knew how to relax and let down its hair.

Customarily in time for the July Fourth hop, the Summer Girls would begin arriving. These young women, from prominent Southern families, were escorted by mothers, aunts or friends and stayed with faculty wives or widows. They attended campus events such as dances, choral and orchestral concerts, debates and varsity athletic contests. A much anticipated occasion for a student was a moonlight stroll around campus with a Summer Girl.

Spirited competition, usually in athletic events, among the dormitories helped relieve the tedium of study.

So did student pranks common to all campuses.

Alvin W. Skardon, Class of '98, told his son that when he was at Sewanee, medical students would dress up their cadavers and place them in lifelike poses at the windows of Thompson Hall to frighten freshmen.

A favorite caper in those years was stretching wire low across a campus path, from tree to tree or post, especially in places where unobservant strollers risked pitching headlong into mud puddles.

As related later in this text, the Iron Men football players were much aware that variety was the spice of college life. Yearbook photographs and texts attest to this. In contrast to football-only players at some schools, Sewanee gridders joined fraternities and secret (fun) societies, performed with choral and orchestral groups, were active in medical, legal, theological and dramatic clubs and competed in sports other than football, such as baseball, golf, tennis and gymnastics.

Even so, despite their long hours of football practice and road trips, they maintained high classroom marks. Sewanee required them to maintain at least a B average.

As a prelude to the football story, I searched 1899 and 1900 campus publications for an on-the-scene description of student life at that time. I found it in a somewhat lengthy, unsigned article in the 1900 *Cap and Gown*. Sewanee sources believe the author was Huger Wilkinson Jervey of Charleston, S.C., who was to become dean of the Columbia University School of International Law. Jervey was described as perhaps the most brilliant student of his day.

My thanks to the university for permission to reprint excerpts.

The Sewanee of To-Day

Sewanee life is too elusive in its charm to be caught with an amateur pencil, has too much of the breath of heaven to be fastened to paper with dull lead. Even the boldest could only hope to give a faint suggestion of its sweetness.

Sewanee, just after Commencement, undergoes a reaction. Things are dull; the dances are over and football practice won't start for six weeks. (Editor's note: *Formal* practice, that is.) A mild form of "girling" is still possible; the Commencement tide of picture-hats and fluffy dresses ebbs slowly. Although the college girl is a *sine qua non* of college life, and although Sewanee without Sewanee girls would not be Sewanee at all, philosophical reflection on their departure might show, in some measure, that it is just as well we do not have them with us always. They are too disturbingly charming. It is after they leave that the men, thrown on each other's mercies during idle hours, learn to know and love one another and forge that mighty chain that binds Sewanee men together with an everlasting bond.

Oh! the joys of those evenings in a neighbor's room. The viands may be primitive—"dog," pimolas, crackers and cheese—but it isn't the details that count, it isn't the food or the dress that we think of—the charm of the freedom, the unreserve, the *abandon*, the collarless oblivion to care, the songs and jokes and heated arguments, the mutual memories of the past, the mutual resolutions for the future, the confidences that are so sweet because they mean so much, the vital pleasure in true friendship's presence—these things make college life the warmest, sunniest, truest, heartiest existence in this world. In these little forums of the "careless drift of college chat," everything from girls and football to politics and religion is discussed. Here the sentiment of the University is formed and the conduct of the officials condemned or applauded. These are the hearthstones, the family potboilings; all of them together make up the University itself.

Sewanee is one of the most democratic places on earth. The absence of any class-system and the mutual dependence of the students on each other for all their amusements and associations break down all barriers of age and money. There is no such thing as financial popularity here, and the snob is not tolerated, because there are no bootlicks to pay him caddish court. The man who has money spends it as freely as he wishes, but his inseparable chum may be living on a scholarship and forced to count the baseball games he can afford to go see.

It is about the first of October that the thump of the football is heard in the land, and from then until the end of the term those who are not trying for the team watch the practice all afternoon and discuss football half the night. Politics and the new books have lost their interest, and arguments about the respective speed of the half-backs, the punting ability of the full-back, the excellence of this year's coach, speculations and criticisms form the subject of the excited conversation of groups of two's and three's in Andy's Alley between classes, at the Supply Store, and in the rooms of every loafer of any consequence in college.

Everybody goes to see the games—the V.C. (Editor: vice-chancellor or president) attends with the same regularity with which he goes to chapel, and the great and the small rub elbows along the side lines, unconscious of all official distinctions, all hearts and minds intent on that little sphere of pigskin which unites all the incongruous elements among the on-lookers into one great fraternity of eager, shouting Sewanee enthusiasts watching the ball carried nearer and nearer the tall, slim goal-posts where lie victory and glory greater than any king or emperor ever battled for and won.

But now only the half has been told. Victory must be celebrated; and in the past two years we have had so many victories that the lesson of celebration we have learned by heart. The night of the '99 football demonstration, when we had won the championship of the South, is an illuminated page in Sewanee's history. You could have read a newspaper out at Morgan Steep by the glare of the bonfires. Forensic was almost rent asunder by the positively fiendish yells of five hundred devils incarnate (this includes the ladies of the mountain); some people spoke, but more people cheered—all of them reiterated two thousand times that Simkins and Suter and "Burrhus" and the whole team and everything connected with it were altogether and entirely right, and when everybody had yelled so much that they were too happy for words, they went home, voiceless and content, to consume throat-tablets so as to be in good voice for the next performance. Sewanee enthusiasm is proverbial—as much so as her poverty.

There is an atmosphere of mental culture in Sewanee. It would hardly be possible for the veriest hoodlum to stay four years at Sewanee without absorbing a certain amount of literary and social *savoir faire*, without getting that distinctive hall-mark of the Sewanee man, which is nothing more nor less than the impress of good manners and good morals and good minds upon him. Not that every man whose feet have trod our streets becomes, *ipso facto*, a gentleman, a Christian and a scholar (that were a rash boast, even for one who loves Sewanee much to make), but the man who is once bitten by a Sewanee tick and innoculated with the spirit of the place, if he does not practice all the virtues and spend his days in searching the Scriptures, at least has a wholesome respect for the man who does, and this gives greater promise for his future. The worst rake in college will discuss the sermon intelligently, and more or less appreciatively, at Sunday dinner-table.

The Vanderbilt debate is just as vital a matter to the well-rounded student as the Vanderbilt football game, and the open meetings of Sigma Epsilon and Pi Omega are largely attended. The man who can "do something" is the big man here, and those who have reached the thirty-third degree of Sewanee immortality have usually been men of more or less intellect.

There is a deep-flowing, an abiding religious influence in the University, not obtrusive or on the surface, but yet a real force working for the good and the true. The Junior who talks a great deal will tell you how much he wishes complusory Chapel (i.e., all Chapel) were abolished, but a Senior realizes that outside of all religious claims the ten-minute morning service in St. Augustine's is the main-spring of University life. The whole college—indeed the whole population of the mountain—assembles there, and the corporate sense, the *esprit de corps* of Sewanee, has its being in this daily contact between each student and the whole University. Chapel is so essentially a student enterprise, as it were, that each man feels it belongs to him, and by and by its religious significance is revealed to him and driven home without his under-standing the process. The Chaplain and the Vice Chancellor were students but yesterday, the choir and the organist are students. Notices of ball games and mass-meetings, and tennis tournaments and germans are given out here. Here the Red Ribbon Society declares publicly whom it has taken unto itself by marching them up the aisle and out of the north transept door, just before the Proctors declare Chapel adjourned. The surest proof that Chapel is a vital institution is the fact that if a man stays away from it for a few weeks, he finds himself falling out of the run of things. He loses interest in the affairs of the University, and his Sewanee spirit is in serious danger.

The return in March is an occasion of rejoicing. Dress-suit cases come up much heavier than they went down. Everybody is so glad to see everybody else that you forget who your last term's enemies were and grasp hands with reckless good fellowship. Those March hand-shakes are always to be remembered. In their hearty sincerity is to be found the true inwardness of the Sewanee Spirit: no mouth-honor, no Judas kisses spoil the straightforward, outspoken, "I am glad to see you." For you are, you are glad to see the proctors and Dr. Richardson and the mail-carrier and Frank. In a few days you settle down to your old crowd and your old ways, but just at first the whole world is your best friend, and you would be quite willing to give your last cent to the treasurer of the Missionary Society. So scrupulously jealous are you of the rights of human kind that, after registering in the Vice Chancellor's office, your delicate consideration for the repose of the proctor is really touching.

The mountain is half empty until June, and then the fuss and feathers begin. Up to the first of June we further the designs of our founders, who thought that Sewanee would be "sequestered from the various temptations attending a promiscuous converse with the world, that theatre of folly and dissipation," but we are too irresist-ible; the world will not stay away from us, and we keep open house for "folly and dissipation" all summer. There are amusements to suit all tastes—addresses by the most eminent bishops in the church—they are as common as deacons in Sewanee—any quantity of Chapel services, History of Art lectures, Oratorical contests, Glee Club concerts, and then the germans. Anyone, male, female, or jonah, who has ever danced on Forensic floor will tell you there's magic to it; so wanderers return from distant lands summer after summer to dance those germans.

Commencement Day itself is splendid in its procession of bishops, trustees and professors, all dressed in a height of academic foppishness, with gowns and silken hoods. To the Junior it is a day of much weariness to the flesh—he has to sit on a hard bench all morning and hear degrees conferred in Greek or Russian or something, and listen to a ponderous dissertation by some notability on the generality of things in general. But to the Senior about to be graduated, it all has a real significance. It means the consummation of his toil and the realization of his hopes and prayers. It also means good-bye to the dearest associations of his life. Yet no—not quite good-bye, after all. Although the whilom college boy is now a grave alumnus and feels the dust of life's highway already choking him, he knows he never will forget.

Sometimes, when the burden is hardest to bear, a mountain breeze and a whispering of leaves will come to him, and his soul will be refreshed by a breath from the good days when hope was buoyant and love rang true. Sewanee "lives always in the heart and life"—for its spirit endureth forever.

Mountaintop jubilee

The homecoming train finally came into view on the mountainside: two wood-burning locomotives laboring the last mile of a steep grade, one pulling, the other pushing a Pullman sleeping car.

Aboard the car were 21 football players with their coach, manager and trainer, returning to the little university town of Sewanee in south central Tennessee.

The year was 1899. The football team was from the University of the South, an Episcopal Church institution known familiarly then and now as Sewanee.

Waiting at the railroad station were hundreds of supporters, including virtually all of the 326-man student body. The team was returning from a 2,500-mile trip to Texas, Louisiana and western Tennessee during which it defeated five major opponents in six days, scoring 91 points while holding all five opponents scoreless.

.The trip was then and ranks today as one of the truly remarkable feats in all sportsdom.

Now the bobtailed train had pulled up at the station and the players were stepping off the Pullman into a tumultuous welcome. After acknowledging the welcome and stretching their travel-weary legs, they were ushered onto a hack, a two-horse carriage—without horses on this occasion—for a victory ride. Jubilant classmates attached ropes to the hack and pulled it a half mile uphill to the campus. There the celebrating continued long into the night, capped with fireworks and a bonfire.

Five days after the team's return, in its Monday, Nov. 21 issue, the campus *Sewanee Purple*, under a heading "THE CELEBRATION—Most Enthusiastic Welcome Sewanee Ever Offered," busted all the buttons off its vest:

No other team in the country since the history of football was written ever played five games in six days and won them all, and all with zeros at the right end, and no team was ever welcomed with a more wildly enthusiastic welcome than that which greeted our returning heros last Wednesday afternoon and evening. Sewanee outdid herself, as the occasion demanded.

To begin at the beginning: The limping, laurel-wreathed lions arrived on the one o'clock train—this doesn't mean that the train came at one p.m., not at all, that's just a nickname employed for convenience's sake; we don't know its origin, probably sarcasm though. But that is by-the-way.

The lions came, were fed, given a little exercise, and then caged and paraded down the street. And a circus it was. The procession formed in front of the Hoffman (medical school dorm) at seven. The scene looked like a fancy dress ball at a home for mental cripples.

The Meds were there in all the eerie and ghoulish splendor of skulls, skeletons and sheets. St. Luke's (the seminary) turned out to a man, was distinctly evangelical in dress and voice, but showed high-church tendencies when it came to the fireworks.

The Law School was brilliant for once, with a transparency borne by President Scott, of the Law Club.

The Academic Department, the backbone, and we might add, the lungs of the University, yelled, and then yelled, and finally yelled a little more. The Grammar School (boarding school) caddied for them, and yelled when they got tired.

Appropriate music was furnished by the Registrar's drum and fife corps of 10 pieces, and by the Bobtown Band.

You could have read a copy of the Sewanee Purple *out on Morgan Steep by the light of the bonfires, Japanese lanterns and torches.*

During the afternoon great stacks of wood had been piled up in front of the Hoffman, Thompson Hall and the grammar School dormitory, and the poor old moon, although just as full as anybody in the crowd, was quite eclipsed.

The twenty-two gods were placed in two triumphal cars, the various departments fell in line, and the procession started. Down the street to the Grammar School dormitory it wound, and the light and the noise grew greater.

Back to Forensic then, and here the whole Mountain was assembled. Mr. Wiggins (Editor: vice-chancellor, president) presided. Mr. McVeigh Harrison spoke for the student body,

Capt. Seibels spoke for the team, Manager Lea spoke for the trunks, and Coach Suter spoke for ten minutes and captivated the audience. Everybody else spoke for himself, and in the loudest tone at his command, so that Forensic (Hall) echoed to the Varsity yells the like of which had never been heard before even in Sewanee.

Enthusiasm like this is infectious; everybody caught it; an insensate Indoo idol would have broadened his smile and gone mad with the college spirit. Oh! it was great. It lasted for an hour or more, and the mob, having gotten all the noise possible out of their voices, had recourse to gunpowder. They adjourned to the Hoffman campus, and skyrockets sizzled, and Roman-candles sputtered, and cannon-crackers exploded, until a late hour.

The whole celebration was right royal in design and execution, and the arrangement committee is to be congratulated for the way in which they made the reception worthy of the received.

Had Abe Lincoln been in the welcome-home crowd, he might have recycled a Gettysburg line thusly: "The world will little note but long remember." That's how things turned out.

Newspapers of that day can be forgiven for little noting. The football sun still rose and set over the Ivy League, far to the northeast, as it had for football's first three decades. A few schools outside the Ivy were getting occasional mention in the press, but Walter Camp, "the father of American football" and chief chronicler of sports news then, seemed either unaware or unimpressed by events south of the Mason-Dixon Line.

The *New York Times,* emerging as the nation's most prestigious newspaper, apparently was just beginning to sense the public's appetite for sports news. If the *Times* had a sports correspondent down South, where football had taken hold in the early 1890s, he was asleep at the switch. A cursory check of the *Times* the week Sewanee came home from its marathon trip found no mention of the five games in six days.

Some Southern papers, particularly those in the cities where Sewanee played the five games, carried accounts of the individual games but apparently didn't recognize the significance of the five games in six days as all that big a deal.

Again, understanding and forgiveness are in order. Football schedules had not settled into their Saturdays-only pattern. You played when your school and another could agree on a date. If that meant two games within five days or even three days, so be it. If, for example, Sewanee had a date to play Georgia in Atlanta and Georgia Tech was available for a game in Atlanta two or three days later, why not stay over, double up and take more gate money home? If the starters got banged up against Georgia, the trainer could rub them down, soothe their aches and wish them well against Tech. After all, then as now, football wasn't for sissies.

Chances are, if wheeler-dealer manager Luke Lea could have had another crack at the five-games-in-six-days event, he probably would have alerted newspapers as to what was happening. For some reason, he missed that opportunity.

When Sewanee played on through its 12-game schedule undefeated, the little mountaintop university did win modest comment, but that was more for being the South's No. 1 team than for the marathon trip.

Even Walter Camp tipped his hat to Sewanee in his preseason outlook for 1900 in *Outing* magazine, the *Sports Illustrated* of its day. But trees obscured the forest for Camp, also. The five wins in six days went unrecognized. Only decades of once-a-week football would put the Iron Men trip in focus.

But the prophet was not without honor at home. The *Sewanee Purple*, which had cheered the team without ceasing since its opening victory, now called on the world to stop and recognize a feat not likely to be matched—ever. History has vindicated the *Purple's* pride.

Sample excerpts from the *Purple* near season's end in '99:

It is undoubtedly true that triumphs boasted of rob them of their virtue, but it also is a recognized principle that circumstances alter cases. That we are entitled to toast the team of '99 the records will show, for have not the sturdy sons of the old Mountain planted Sewanee's banner in the Temple of Fame, and ere darkness sets in on Thanksgiving Day will we not hail them as champions of the South?

The Varsity's achievements are unparalleled, and all honor and praise are due the men who have striven so conscientiously for their alma mater and established a record in the annals of football which will remain unequaled for many generations. No other eleven, east, west, north or south, can boast of ten successive victories with a goal line uncrossed by an opponent. (Editor's note: Auburn later scored the season's only points on Sewanee, but the men in purple defeated Auburn and North Carolina in their final two games.)

—

In all probability it will remain the trip for many years to come.

—

Our duty to posterity demands that we duly record in print that shall never die the achievements of these twenty-three brave souls (Editor's note: Referring to the 21 players plus coach and manager) who drew a Purple line all through the Southland, and claimed five winning footballs for their own and for Sewanee. The story might read like an epic poem if it had not become prosy to us through the dint of repetition, but the world must know, and those yet unborn must know what mighty things Sewanee can do and has done, and so they are writ here.

That remarkable season with its 12 victories, five of them coming in six days, is worth exploring.

First up: Introducing the 24 people aboard the Pullman special who rode west into history.

II

Iron Men roll call

Had a passenger from another car strolled through the '99 Sewanee squad's private Pullman, the stroller might never have guessed he or she was among football players.

Yearbook pictures indicate the players were clean-cut, handsome types. A few of the linemen might have provided an athletes tipoff, but as a group the young men could have passed as college students on a field trip. Many kept textbooks beside them, both to stay abreast in class and to help fill the long travel hours.

In the last years of the 19th century, as football spread from the prestigious Ivy League, the quality of player personnel dipped, sometimes markedly.

On occasion, "student" players at some schools went through the motions of enrolling, then stayed around campus for football only. Others didn't bother even with the motions. At one football-happy institution several key players reportedly never enrolled and never went near a classroom.

An observer of the college scene in those years wrote that on many campuses, players were viewed as "crude, muscular mugs, not worthy of attention from people of breeding and culture."

In contrast, consider the makeup of the Sewanee squad that made the 2,500-mile road trip and won the five games in six days. Of the 21 players making the trip, five were law students; four, medical; four, theological, and the remainder academic. Their average age was just over 21 and average weight 169, according to a *Montgomery Advertiser* story just prior to the Sewanee-Auburn game played Thanksgiving Day 1899.

No football-only types, these. Fifteen would go on to earn degrees (14 at Sewanee), and almost all would go on to success in chosen professions, as a later chapter will detail.

Three decades after the Iron Men trip, in a radio talk the night before the 1931 Sewanee-Auburn game, '99 team captain Diddy Seibels would have this to say: "To what was Sewanee's brilliant success due? I attribute it to one thing alone and it is the greatest thing any team can have: teamwork. There was about that team an esprit de corps that was truly wonderful. Like the Three Musketeers, their motto was 'One for all and all for one.'

"Discipline was perfect. There were no jealousies, only the indomitable will to win, that unconquerable never-say-die Sewanee spirit, the same spirit that won for us in the championship game against North Carolina."

Introductions of the about-to-be Iron Men, along with their coach, manager and trainer, are in order.

Billy Suter, coach

Born in Greensburg, Pa., Herman Milton "Billy" Suter played football for two schools—Washington & Jefferson and Penn State—before enrolling at Princeton. He became a star athlete at Princeton despite weighing only 140 or so. He captained the baseball team as a senior and excelled as an outfielder in the spring of 1899.

Noted sports columnist Grantland Rice, whose path was to cross Suter^s in later years, recalled that Suter once ran for a 95-yard touchdown against Harvard. That was some feat, considering that most running gains in those days (the mid and late '90s) were ground out through the line a yard or two at a time.

With Suter as senior quarterback, Princeton won all its 1898 games except against Cornell, which edged the Tigers 5-0.

After the 1898 Sewanee season when Coach J.G. "Lady" Jayne, also a Princetonian, was hired away by North Carolina, Jayne reportedly recommended Suter, with whom he had roomed at Princeton, as his successor. Jayne apparently convinced Luke Lea, the incoming student manager at Sewanee, that Suter could win there.

Columnist Rice was on three Vanderbilt baseball teams that played Suter-coached Sewanee teams. Decades later he wrote that Suter, with his keen spirit and thorough knowledge of both baseball and football, was a natural leader. His players believed in him and he in his players, Rice wrote, "yet he was one of the strictest disciplinarians I've ever known."

Luke Lea, manager

Born into a pioneer Tennessee family prominent in politics and law, Lea participated in numerous Sewanee activities, including publications, and earned a bachelor of arts degree in the spring of 1899, then stayed another year to earn a master's.

Whether he sought out the job of student manager of the football team or was asked to take it isn"t clear, but because he was a man of action, it seems likely he was self-appointed, one account says. Sewanee historiographer Arthur Ben Chitty described Lea as "a negotiating genius."

The way American football evolved, for many years the team captain was on almost even footing with the coach, who often was viewed as an adviser. At Sewanee in 1899 Lea made it a triumvirate—coach, captain, manager. For all intents and purposes Lea was athletic director; as such, he began putting together the schedule that would land Sewanee in the record books for all time.

Lea's first target was Vanderbilt, which had beaten Sewanee in eight of the 11 games they had played since their intense rivalry had begun in 1891 (the down-the-road neighbors sometimes played twice a season). Apparently Lea felt that Sewanee wasn't getting a large enough share of the gate receipts and the disagreement resulted in the '99 game being canceled, if indeed it ever was formally scheduled.

Loss of the Vandy-game revenue may have started Lea's wheels spinning toward compensation from a more ambitious schedule. In any case, the early-season schedule as published in the *Purple* did not include the five games in six days.

The Sewanee squad acquired new uniforms for '99 and Lea probably had a hand in the acquisition. The '99 manager was not one to sit on his hands, then or in later life.

Cal Burrows, trainer

Long before team physicians, whirlpool baths and such, Burrows was therapist and healer at Sewanee, a kneader of sore muscles, bruised knees and tired bodies.

Burrows probably had no training to become trainer, but learned by doing. With four medical students on the squad, he had access to advice about rubdowns and treating injuries. That Burrows made the 2,500-mile week-long road trip makes clear his value to the football program.

Henry Goldthwaite "Diddy" Seibels, right halfback and captain

Two sons, Henry G. Seibels Jr. ("Buzz" to friends) and Kelly Seibels said the oddball nickname "Diddy" (sometimes spelled "Ditty") probably came either from his early attempts to say "daddy" or from relatives' baby talk as they bounced him on their knees.

In boyhood days on Montgomery's South Perry Street, Diddy was gung-ho for baseball. He showed talent as a pitcher and once ran away with a semi-pro team, Buzz recalled his father telling him. Diddy's mother was described as being totally opposed to her son's playing baseball until she learned that professional players made good money.

Diddy attended Starke military school not far from his home, then, as older brother Temple had done a few years earlier, enrolled at Sewanee. The opportunity to play college baseball or the still-new game of football may have attracted him there, along with the availability of quality education for a bargain price.

Seibels was on the Board of Editors, was president of the Sewanee Athletic Association, and a member of the German Club and Law Club.

A versatile athlete, Seibels participated in several sports, including baseball and golf, but football ultimately got most of his attention and time. He liked the physical challenge of tackling and blocking, and his speed quickly won him notice as a breakaway runner.

Once against Georgia Tech, Buzz recalled, Diddy returned a kickoff for a touchdown, but Sewanee was whistled for an infraction, probably offside, and the run was nullified. Sewanee players were unhappy about the run being called back, but Seibels, confident and a little cocky, quieted them with a promise to repeat the touchdown runback on the second kickoff. He kept the promise.

As the 1899 season approached, Seibels, a liberal arts student who had shown leadership potential, was chosen captain. As noted earlier, in those years team captains were on almost equal footing with head coaches. Thus, Diddy encouraged teammates to make all practices, to work into top physical condition, to put team effort above individual. In game action he would make many decisions without counsel from the sidelines.

Buzz recalled that his dad, although "reluctant to talk about past glory," had told him and Kelly about preparations for the five-games-in-six-days trip. His principal exhortation to teammates was, "Don't get hurt!" There was ample reason: If a player left a game at any point for any reason, rules of the day forbade the player reentering the game.

"Then in the very first game on that trip, against Texas, Daddy got his head busted," Buzz said. But game accounts related that the gash on Diddy's forehead was held together with "sticking plaster," and he played all the way, scoring both Sewanee touchdowns. He missed only the Tulane game.

Ormond Simkins, fullback

Should Hollywood decide one day to make a movie of Sewanee's marathon trip, Simkins' role would be a leading one.

His father, William Stewart Simkins, was a South Carolinian who, by one account, fired the first shot of the War Between the States. His obituary in an Austin, Tex., newspaper corrected that, quoting Ormond's father that he only helped load the gun that fired the first shot on Fort Sumter.

The elder Simkins moved to Florida, where he practiced law, then on to Corsicana, Tex., where Ormond was born and spent part of his boyhood. Later the family moved to Austin where the father joined the University of Texas law school faculty and authored law books.

Ormond Simkins entered Sewanee in 1896 and eventually earned a BA degree (1902). In baseball he was catcher and team captain. He was president of the campus Texas Club and in the German and Glee clubs.

Teammate Seibels later would tell his sons that Simkins, not he, was Sewanee's best player. Newspaper accounts confirm that Simkins indeed was versatile. Like Seibels, he relished physical contact. He blocked and tackled well, ran the ball for frequent sizable gains and contributed much to Sewanee game plans with what one fan, in a letter years later, called long, beautiful spiral punts.

In a 1944 interview with columnist Grantland Rice, Coach Suter described Simkins as "one of the greatest football players I ever saw, a fine kicker, a fine ball carrier and the most terrific tackler and blocker I've ever seen."

Play-by-play accounts in later chapters show how valuable the 5-foot-10 Simkins was to Sewanee. Still another chapter, following up on the Iron Men after Sewanee days, tells of the tragedy, resulting from leg injuries, that dogged Simkins the rest of his life.

Ringland Fisher "Rex" Kilpatrick, left halfback

From Bridgeport, Ala., Rex Kilpatrick was a younger brother of Yale football star John Reed Kilpatrick, but Rex chose to play at nearby Sewanee. The Kilpatricks had moved from New York to Bridgeport, where their father was a real estate investor. The little town nestled in northeast Alabama close to Chattanooga was being promoted as a site for industry and home sites.

At 6-feet-1 and 185 pounds, Rex was one of the heavier players on the '99 team. He started all but one of the five games in six days and contributed much in ball-carrying and tackling. Although ends Bartlet Sims and Bunny Pearce attempted most of Sewanee's points-after-touchdowns, Kilpatrick would play a hero's role by kicking the winning field goal against North Carolina.

Rex entered law school in 1899, was a member of the German Club and president of the campus Alabama Club. In addition to playing football, he pitched for the baseball team and was a member of the German and Law clubs. He did not earn a degree at Sewanee.

William Blackburn "Warbler" Wilson, quarterback

Some accounts of the 1899 team say Manager Luke Lea "scoured the South" recruiting the best players he could find for Sewanee. Perhaps so, but historiographer Arthur Ben Chitty doesn't think so. He insists that Sewanee didn't have to recruit with scholarship offers, that the university was such an education bargain that players sought out Sewanee.

One exception was "Warbler" (also called "Black" and "Blackie") Wilson. He had played one season as second-string quarterback for the University of South Carolina in 1896 and was working in his father's law office in Rock Hill, S.C., when—according to a Herman Helms column in the *Charlotte Observer*—Lea contacted him.

(The Helms interview with Wilson makes clear that Lea had a hand in Sewanee football before he became manager for the '99 team.)

According to Helms, Lea told Wilson that Sewanee was "filled with football ambition" and wanted him to play quarterback. Reportedly offered a full scholarship covering tuition and other expenses, Wilson accepted. Among his campus activities, he was a member of the Law Club.

At 5-feet-10, "Warbler" weighed only 132 pounds in 1897 and 142 in 1898, but by the 1899 season he had grown to 154 and by 1900, when he would be team captain, to 168. He told Helms that he suffered a broken leg against Vanderbilt in the 1898 game, but the Sewanee trainer "bandaged" him and he played the rest of the way, 45 more minutes, helping lead teammates to a 19-4 victory.

Wilson was very much a key to success on the Iron Men trip. As quarterback he called out play numbers (there were no pre-play huddles as yet), the numbers signaling which player would carry the ball and where he would hit the line. The quarterback had to take the snap from center, then would hand off or pitch the ball to a runner.

Bartlet et Ultimus Sims, left end

Despite being a dependable starter on the '99 team, Sims was not often mentioned in game reports. In the early games of the Texas trip, he was Sewanee's placekicker on points-after-touchdowns. The fact that he hung tough at end game after game convinced Suter he deserved a starting spot.

Sims was from Bryan, Tex., which meant he was playing against homefolks when Sewanee met Texas A&M in Houston in the second game of the marathon trip. He was 6-feet-tall and weighed 185, large enough at end to be a strong blocker and tackler.

Presumably, Sims' parents tacked the "et Ultimus" onto his name to signify he would be the caboose, their last child.

John William Jones, left tackle

A native of Marshall, Tex., Jones had earned a BA degree at Roanoke College in Virginia before enrolling as a theological student at Sewanee. He was not timid about expressing his feelings, according to an article in the *Purple*. Apparently either written by or contributed to by manager Luke Lea, the article noted that "Jones swore a lot" on the Texas trip.

Stories in the *Purple* did not carry bylines, but because Lea kept the student paper informed by telegraph about the trip, chances are he wrote the recap of the trip, including the comment about Jones.

In addition to making Sewanee's line tough to penetrate, Jones occasionally was called on to carry the ball (legal then) and he made sizable gains, as the play-by-play accounts will show.

He was an essay medalist and associate editor of the *Sewanee Literary Magazine*.

Henry Sheridan Keyes, left guard

From Cambridge, Mass., and a medical student, at 205

Keyes was a bulwark in the Sewanee line.

William Henry Poole, center

A 6-footer weighing 185, Poole was responsible on offense for snapping the ball to the quarterback and on defense for standing firm against thrusts through the line. A theology major, he was from Glyndon, Md. A student orator, he served on the University's Board of Editors, was a German Club member, president of the Pan-Hellenic Convention and associate editor of the *Sewanee Literary Magazine.*

Another Luke Lea line in the *Purple* reported that Poole "drank heavily" on the squad's one off-day on the trip. If true, either Poole played against LSU the next day with a doozy of a hangover or his "heavy drinking" consisted of a couple of beers.

William Stirling Claiborne, right guard

This 190-pound 6-footer from Amherst County, Va., believed that pre-game intimidation of opposing players would make them easier to handle in the line of scrimmage.

At an unspecified time before the big trip, more likely much earlier in his life, he had lost the vision in one eye, and now he made the most of the loss. Facing opposing players before each game, he would point to the discolored eye and proclaim, "I got this last time out!"

Before enrolling at Sewanee to study theology, Claiborne had attended Roanoke College in 1893-95, so he truly was a senior player. He was a member of the Missionary Society and vice president of the Athletic Association.

Richard Elliott Bolling, right tackle

Playing alongside Claiborne, this 5-foot-10 medical student from Edna, Tex., helped make the right side of Sewanee's line difficult to penetrate.

Hugh Miller Thompson "Bunny" Pearce, right end

A tough little guy from Jackson, Miss., Pearce was listed at 125 and 5-feet-3. In recounting the '99 season to Grantland Rice in 1944, Coach Suter remembered Pearce as weighing only 114, but Sewanee records indicate Pearce was at least 10 pounds heavier. No matter, as Suter told Rice, most of whatever Pearce weighed was "brains and heart."

The bantamweight attempted most of Sewanee's points-after-touchdowns on the Texas trip.

Pearce played in the University Orchestra and was on the gymnastics team.

The substitutes

Only three or four of the 10 reserves who made the trip saw much game action, but newspaper game stories made it clear virtually all made at least brief appearances.

Ralph Peters Black, end, 158, 6 feet, was born in Sylvania, Ga., and reared in Atlanta. A liberal arts student, he was in the German, Chess and Tennis clubs.

Preston Smith Brooks, Jr., of Sewanee, a liberal arts student and member of the gymnastics team, was a grandson of a South Carolina congressman, also Preston Brooks, who publicly caned Massachusetts Sen. Charles Sumner in pre-Civil War days. Sumner had criticized Carolina Sen. Andrew Pickens Butler, absent from the Senate that day, and Brooks took offense.

Harris Goodwin Cope, of Savannah, Ga., was a law student. At 16 he had weighed less than 100; in football togs he finally made it up to 117. Cope was an outfielder in baseball and a member of the Law, German, Golf and Tennis clubs.

Andrew Cleveland Evins of Spartanburg, S.C., "would wax loquacious" on the trip, according to Luke Lea's account. Evins was a liberal arts student.

Daniel Baldwin Hull, 5-10 160-pounder from Savannah, was a law student who aspired to writing stories of the outdoors. He also played baseball and was a member of the Golf and German clubs.

Joseph Lee Kirby-Smith, born in Sewanee in 1882, was a son of a former Confederate general. In liberal arts, he would enter Medical School in 1903.

Landon Randolph Mason, a medical student, was from Marshall, Va. He was a member of the campus Medical/Surgical Society.

Floy Hoffman Parker was a liberal arts student from Canton, Miss.

Albert T. Davidson of Augusta, Ga., in liberal arts, was a German Club member.

Charles Quintard Gray was a liberal arts student from Ocala, Fla. He was a tenor in the University Choir and treasurer of the Glee Club, played cello in the orchestra, was president of the Florida Club, and in the Golf and German clubs.

Because no 1899 roster was found, an accurate count of players who had to be left at home was not possible, but a guess would be six or eight. Among them was a freshman, Herbert E. Smith, once mistakenly listed in an article by this writer as having made the trip. Lea and Suter had to be guided by how many men they would need, balanced by how many they could afford to take.

III

The way they played the game

efore they boarded their Pullman special Tuesday, Nov. 7, 1899, the Sewanee football players browsing the Sunday *New York Times* could have read that

—*Boer military forces had been driven from two key positions as war continued in South Africa.*
—*Admiral George Dewey, still basking in his naval triumph over the Spanish navy in Manila Bay, attracted hero-worshipers as he strolled New York streets with his bride-to-be.*
—*Cuban demonstrators pressed their case for independence from the United States, which recently had taken over the island from Spain.*
—*A New York express wagon ran over and killed a young woman bicyclist.*
—*Favorites won at the Aqueduct horse race track.*
—*Princeton and Pennsylvania football squads (and others, of course) practiced for upcoming games.*

If the *Times* sports desk had been alerted that a little known Tennessee mountaintop football squad was departing Tuesday to travel 2,500 miles and play five games in six days, the news did not appear in the *Times* that Sunday. (Could that have been a public relations oversight on manager/promoter Luke Lea's part?)

On that 1899 Sunday, William McKinley was in the White House after having defeated William Jennings Bryan in 1896. Vice President Garet Hobart lay seriously ill that day; he would die a week after the Sewanee team returned home.

The Union now was comprised of 45 states; Oklahoma, New Mexico and Arizona would join early in the new century, Alaska and Hawaii much later.

Automobiles were still a novelty to be stared at in astonishment; McKinley became in 1899 the first president to ride in a car, a Stanley Steamer. The Wright brothers were preparing their "airplane" in an Ohio shop for trial flight at Kitty Hawk, N.C., in 1903.

Aspirin, which had been around a long time, was introduced in this country as a "modern" drug.

If in 1899 you planned out-of-town travel, you bought a train ticket. If you would be traveling overnight, you could pay extra and sleep in a Pullman berth. That touch of comfort was especially tempting if you were going 2,500 miles to play five football games in six days.

A fortunate few people had telephones. Almost every family had a buggy and/or a wagon. And if you wanted to send messages back home while on the road, as during a football trip, you went to the nearest telegraph office.

With the 20th century at hand (some people would argue it was more than a year away), various sports were mushrooming, especially baseball, football and basketball.

Baseball had caught on in earnest after the War Between the States and football was not far behind. After starting in 1891, basketball was becoming popular.

College football began with the Rutgers-Princeton game in 1869. For a few years the game was largely a blend of rugby and soccer, bearing little resemblance to football as we know it today. Then a remarkable young athlete named Walter Camp showed up at Yale in 1876, first as player, then coach, official, rules maker, rules interpreter, administrator and author. He would become known as "the father of American football."

Camp brought order, strategy and limited open play to a game that had bogged down in pushing, shoving, slugging and mass-play confusion. He established the line of scrimmage, 11 men to a side, yards-to-gain for a first down, and this scoring: 2 points for a touchdown, 4 for a goal after touchdown, 5 for a goal from the field and 1 for a safety. Those point values would change through the years.

Through Camp's influence, tackling below the waist had become legal, and blocking linemen were required to keep arms at their sides instead of extending them.

Players now lined up in formation much like today's instead of spreading across the field.

Even at this pioneer stage of football, names still familiar today came to the fore. Walter Camp leads the list. A sampling of other unforgettables of the game's early days:

—Walter "Pudge" Heffelfinger, Yale's three-time All-American guard, who played every minute of 52 consecutive games, then continued after graduation to play in alumni and all-star games until late in life. At 54, "Pudge" was described by Grantland Rice as "still the greatest guard in the country."

—Amos Alonzo Stagg, who played on the same Yale team and went on to become the winningest coach of all time until late in the 20th century when Alabama's Bear Bryant passed him in total victories.

—John Heisman, who played at both Brown and Penn, then from 1892 until 1927 coached at numerous schools, including Auburn, where he became a stormy chapter in the 1899 Sewanee story. Much later his name would be on the country's best-known football trophy.

—Pat O'Dea, an Australian who played for Wisconsin and earned the title of "greatest kicker of all time." His specialty was said to be 70- and 80-yard punts, but his dropkicks made him famous. He dropkicked a 60-yard field goal against Chicago, a 42-yarder on the run against Minnesota and a 62-yarder against Northwestern in a blizzard.

—Glenn "Pop" Warner of Cornell, who would gain fame as coach of the Carlisle Indians, including Jim Thorpe. "Pop" joined Walter Camp as a football author, once offering a how-to-play correspondence course.

By 1899 the playing field had been redrawn to 110 yards long and 53 1/3 yards wide and was marked with transverse lines every five yards, leading to the description of the field as a "gridiron." The five-yard markers helped officials determine if a team had advanced the ball the then-necessary five yards in three plays for a first down.

A game consisted of two halves of 35 minutes each, but the referee could stop a game because of darkness; presumably that point was agreed on before the game began.

Prior to 1896 the ball had been egg-shaped and leather-covered, a rugby ball. In 1896 it became a "prolate spheroid," looking much more like the ball used today and ideal for dropkicking, which often was used instead of placekicking. For a dropkick, the kicker dropped the ball end-down directly in front of him, and swung his foot into it just as it touched the ground.

Rules now permitted five players on the line of scrimmage and six in the backfield. Two players had to be at least five yards back or outside of the end player on the line. Only one player was permitted in motion before the ball was snapped, and his motion had to be toward his own goal.

In that day, rules apparently provided that a team that scored then would receive, rather than kick off. Presumably, kicking off was considered an advantage over receiving.

Officials consisted of a referee, umpire, linesman and assistant linesman. The latter two frequently were designated from the opposing teams, as the Sewanee game accounts reported.

Newspaper and magazine writeups often referred to the ball being "passed," but the reference was to handoffs and laterals, not to the forward pass that would be approved in 1906.

Early-years player uniforms were factory- or home-made. The following description of a typical uniform appeared in *Outing* magazine:

"(The uniform is) a sleeveless canvas jacket and very loose moleskin or khaki trousers sewed together with an elastic waistband, the whole forming one piece. With this is worn a jersey, stockings and leather shoes with leather cleats nailed to the soles to prevent slipping, and a stiff leather toe-cap, particularly in the case of a kicker."

Just down the football road from 1899 were the forward pass, the coming of such coaches as Fielding "Hurry-up" Yost and Knute Rockne, the rise to prominence of such teams as Notre Dame, Michigan, Army, Illinois, Oklahoma, Auburn, Alabama, Vanderbilt, Georgia Tech and Tennessee. And, yes, Sewanee, the little University of the South. But Sewanee's best-remembered place in football history is the Iron Men trip of 1899.

The years just before, during and just after Sewanee's five-games trip saw many trends, among them: a growing recognition of the value of strong defense and a good kicking game, assumption of more authority by coaches and lessening of authority for team captains, and continued de-emphasis on mass formation plays such as the much-criticized flying wedge.

But as the popularity of football grew, so did criticism of the game's violent nature. Public officials and college administrators alike sought ways of reducing the injuries and rare fatalities that occurred on the "playing" field. Football was not really a *game*, they said, but an exhibition of brute force. Indeed, one historian wrote that if a player wasn't bloody after a game, he was "out of fashion."

When Eastern and Midwestern teams increasingly scheduled games that called for long road trips and the resulting extended absences from classrooms, faculty representatives insisted on a geographical tightening-up.

In 1897 the death of a University of Georgia player led to this editorial comment in the *Birmingham News*:

"The death of a student of the University of Georgia as the result of injuries in a football game in Atlanta Saturday again demonstrates the necessity for abolishing this inhuman sport not only in the schools and colleges, but generally.

"As it is played in this day and generation football is in no sense scientific. It is simply a display of brute force.

"It is more brutal than prize fighting and a greater menace to human life, because a larger number of persons engage in a contest than in a punching match....It is to be hoped that the students will wake to the fact that the future of athletics is seriously threatened."

Thus, in a day when some college leaders were insisting on less travel and more study, and when the public outcry against football was peaking, the 1899 Sewanee football squad departed on a 2,500-mile trip to play five major opponents in six days, a week that would test the players' stamina, physical condition and morale, and certainly risk serious injury.

IV

Sewanee, pre-Iron Age

An intriguing question about the early decades of college football: How did Sewanee, a small, geographically isolated school, gain attention alongside such as Yale, Harvard, Pennsylvania, Auburn, Georgia and Texas? A few solid clues and a tad of speculation suggest the answer.

For a few years after Rutgers and Princeton introduced a game blended of rugby and soccer in 1869, the Ivy League had football to itself. Then gradually other schools in the Northeast and the Midwest got in on the act, and by 1890 or soon thereafter teams in all sections of the country were playing.

Most of the pioneer teams were attached, at least by name, to colleges; others were established by athletic clubs in larger cities. For example, the Birmingham Athletic Club, one of the first to emerge in the South, held its own against colleges and other athletic clubs for a time.

A decade before the 20th century, college football had gained a strong toehold in the Southeast and Southwest. Virginia, Vanderbilt, Georgia, Auburn, Alabama, Tennessee, Tulane, Texas, Texas A&M—a researcher of Southern football would expect those names. But Sewanee? How did the small church school stake an early claim in this roughhouse, sometimes bloody game?

Sewanee's founders (1857) had envisioned an American Oxford, a Southern university dedicated to academic excellence within a Christian environment. The founders' dream, starting with the first students in 1868, materialized; a steady stream of scholars attests to that. But one element the founders couldn't have foreseen was a strong student body urge to compete with other schools in athletics.

Baseball and some minor sports already had caught on at the University of the South when the new game out of the East began getting attention. Students from every department—medical, legal, theological and academic— were caught up in the curiosity about football, and many decided to play despite demanding study requirements.

There is evidence that graduates of Eastern prep schools with football teams introduced the game at Sewanee. An early account notes that two Lawrenceville School former students helped teach the game to Sewanee classmates.

Football became an organized sport at Sewanee in 1890, according to the *Purple*, but the one intercollegiate game arranged that year—with Vanderbilt—was canceled at Vandy's request, so the university's first games were played in 1891. That year Sewanee lost twice to Vandy and defeated the University of Tennessee. Operating without a coach, the team took orders from its captain, as did many other early teams.

In 1892 Sewanee hired a coach, Bowdoin graduate F.G. Sweat, the first of several Purple coaches from the Northeast and the first *paid* coach in the South, according to the *Purple*. Sweat's team defeated five opponents, including Vandy twice, lost to Virginia and tied Louisville Athletic Club.

The next season, which was 3-3, Sewanee lost two games to Vandy, the start of five straight losses to the Commodores, but won its first encounters with Alabama, Auburn and the Birmingham Athletic Club. Coach Sweat filled in at fullback against BAC, something that rules of that time permitted.

A Tufts product, H.C. Foss, took over as coach in 1894. Sewanee played several teams it had not faced before, including North Carolina, Georgia and Tulane, and finished with a 3-4 record.

Yet another coach, R.M. Reynolds of Princeton, was on hand for the 1895 season. His first effort was a 0-0 draw with a strong North Carolina team on Sewanee's Hardee Field. Followup victories over Cumberland and the University of Nashville made the season promising, but Georgia and Vanderbilt spoiled the promise, and the season finished 2-2-1.

J.E. Blair of the University of Pennsylvania coached the '96 team, which had a speedy ball carrier named Henry G. "Diddy" Seibels. After victories over the University of Nashville and Central U. of Kentucky, Sewanee went to Tuscaloosa, Ala., and defeated Alabama 10-6. Then the roof caved in with losses to Georgia, Auburn and Vandy.

Coach Blair departed, passing the reins to J.G. "Lady" Jayne of Princeton, and Jayne's first season was Sewanee's worst since the very first. Ormond Simkins, a Texan who would shine as a member of the '99 team, played left end in '97 as the team slumped to one win, three losses and a tie. But brighter days were ahead.

Simkins moved to fullback and swifty Seibels to right halfback as Sewanee defeated all four opponents it faced in 1898. A yellow fever scare cut the season short, but the team made its first long road trip, to Austin, Tex., where it defeated the University of Texas. Presaging what was to come in '99, Sewanee knocked off arch-rival Vanderbilt at Nashville 19-4, the Commodores' points being the only ones scored on Sewanee that year.

Probably because of the short season, Sewanee's unbeaten year got little attention outside the South (meaning from Walter Camp), but the stage was being set for 1899. The little school on the mountain was about to climb another kind of mountain and pull a feat the football world has never seen equaled.

Sewanee was loading up for '99 with these five factors as ammo:

1. **The quality and commitment of its student/ athletes**. The school's pursuit of academic excellence, along with its isolated campus, helped nurture a family atmosphere and student pride. In contrast to players at many other schools, Sewanee football players were also scholars. More than half earned Sewanee degrees and 15 of the 21 eventually earned degrees at Sewanee or another institution.

2. **A highly advantageous school calendar**. To avoid the winter season when roads often were impassable and almost any transportation to the campus at times impossible, Sewanee scheduled its school year from spring through fall. That meant not only would students be home during the winter, but also as soon as baseball

season ended, the football squad could practice on its own all through the summer. Thus, there were bonus weeks for fine-tuning plays and physical conditioning, a tremendous advantage over teams that had to wait until September to start practice.

3. **Seasoned players**. At most schools player turnover from year to year was a major problem, but going into '99 Sewanee would have most starters back from the unbeaten '98 team. Relating that to modern squads, the benefit doubles because gridders back then played both offense and defense and seldom left a game.

4. **The arrival of Billy Suter as coach**. The departure of "Lady" Jayne to coach at North Carolina normally would have been a setback, but Suter appears to have more than compensated for his departure. According to Grantland Rice, a Vandy student who saw Suter in action as both football and baseball coach, Suter not only was a firm disciplinarian but also was a coach who could motivate his players to peak performance.

5. **The advent of Luke Lea as manager**. Without Lea, almost certainly there would have been no five-games-in-six-days schedule for Sewanee. With someone else as manager, the gate receipts disagreement with Vandy probably would have been resolved and the Sewanee schedule arranged about as in previous seasons. The '99 team had the talent to go through unbeaten and claim the Southern championship, but without the trip Lea set up, Sewanee could not have claimed its unique niche in football history.

The Iron Men were in the wings.

V

Prelude to history

A s Sewanee's 1899 schedule began taking shape, pre-season locker room talk might be imagined.

"Can you believe what they're lining up for us this year?"

"Somebody—Lea or Suter—must have lost his cotton-pickin' mind." Cotton picking was big in those days.

"Just because we're not playing Vandy, does that mean we play a suicide schedule to make up for it?"

In actuality, no whit of evidence exists that the Iron-Men-to-be raised the slightest objection to the marathon schedule being put together for them.

One or two additional games probably would have compensated for the revenue lost because No. 1 rival Vanderbilt wasn't on the schedule. A search for an explanation of the "iron" schedule leads to one person: Luke Lea. Lining up five games in six days reflects the way Lea thought and lived—open the throttle and let 'er rip. That seemed to be his mindset, in sports, business, politics and even war, as a later-chapter look at his post-Sewanee years will show.

Luke Lea, Jr., told me recently that he was certain his father arranged the five games in six days with one purpose in mind: revenue. If Sewanee was to make a long and expensive trip, then it made sense, meaning gate receipts, to play as many games as possible on the trip.

How much leeway did Lea have in arranging the schedule? Full, apparently. Vice Chancellor Lawton Wiggins could have overruled him at any point, but—as a yearbook writer has made clear—Wiggins was an ardent football fan, so apparently he gave Lea full rein.

Did new-coach Billy Suter wince at what Lea was lining up? Circumstantial evidence suggests the opposite, that he relished the challenge.

In its June 20 edition, the *Purple* printed a prospective schedule that included the University of Nashville, Georgia, Tennessee, Texas, Cincinnati and Auburn. No two of the games would be played in the same week. The *Purple* added: "Games will be scheduled with either Louisiana State University and Tulane, or University of Mississippi and University of Alabama, on the Texas trip."

Later the Purple printed this revised schedule: Oct. 21 Georgia at Atlanta, Oct. 23 Georgia Tech at Atlanta, Oct. 28 Tennessee at Sewanee, Nov. 9 Texas at Austin, Nov. 11 Tulane at New Orleans, Nov. 13 LSU at Baton Rouge, Nov. 14 Mississippi (site undecided), Nov. 15 University of Nashville at Sewanee, Nov. 18 Cumberland at Sewanee, Nov. 30 Auburn at Montgomery, Dec. 2 North Carolina at Atlanta.

Thus the five-games-in-six-days schedule now lacked only Texas A&M at Houston Nov. 10, and the resourceful Lea soon attended to that. He added A&M, dropped Nashville and the stage was set.

The appearance of North Carolina on the schedule clears up a point. Some accounts of the Iron Men season suggest that the Carolina game was arranged on short notice, just after Sewanee had defeated Auburn Nov. 30, that Sewanee and Carolina agreed to a challenge game to decide the undisputed championship of the South. Clearly the game in Atlanta was not an 11th-hour matchup. Instead the two schools formally agreed—after Sewanee's win over Auburn—that the winner in Atlanta could claim the championship of the South.

In reviewing the 1898 season, *Outing* magazine in February 1899 had assessed Sewanee's four victories and no defeats. "Sewanee commenced the season with a good nucleus of old players, around which was built a perfect working team full of the same ginger that has always been a feature of her work, but adding to it a knowledge of the game heretofore unknown there. As a perfect machine it was the best in the South, and the record made will be a standard for her to work with in the future."

Then in its November 1899 issue, in an article prepared before the season began, *Outing* reported that Sewanee's preparation had been characterized by "fast work with light material, and under the leadership of Seibels this year will be no exception; their knack of rounding out a championship team from seemingly indifferent material has won the admiration of their rivals. Last year they captured the Vanderbilt colors, and the chances are that Auburn has a very heavy engagement for Thanksgiving."

As usual, Sewanee players had worked into peak condition and had fine-tuned their plays all through the summer, so by the time Suter called them together Sept. 11 they had gotten their customary jump on the teams they would play.

On Sept. 19 the *Purple* reported that "while it is rather early to predict what the season will bring forth, we think that we can safely assert that the team of '99 will not be inferior to its predecessors." As the season demonstrated that was a bit understated.

The first week of practice under Suter's supervision developed two points, the *Purple* said. "First, that we have a good coach—a man who thoroughly understands his business and one who will lend all his energies toward the development of a winning team. Secondly, that we have the material to make such a team."

Suter was invited to report to the student body on the team's progress in practice. He responded with a lengthy, signed article in the *Purple*. Among his comments:

"Several of last year's best players have not returned this fall, but for the vacant places on the team there is good material on hand. Twenty-five men are now in training for the eleven, and during the next few days it is likely this number will be materially increased....

"In the backfield the material is very good, indeed, and there will be a battle royal for the first places. As the schedule is a hard one this year, more mén than usual will be needed for the backfield positions....

"In the development of this year's team the greatest difficulty will be in filling the line positions acceptably. Especially is this true of the ends; while a guard and tackle also are needed, along with a number of substitutes....

"The management is highly gratified by interest taken in football this fall by the medical students, a number of them having gone into training....

"Sewanee is fortunate in having a good captain (Seibels)—a man who already shows decided ability, and who is a hard worker on the field. The management of the team is also in proper hands and is being well directed." (Editor's note: Suter and Lea had hit it off from the start.)

Then Suter referred to the '99 schedule, still being juggled and working toward the five-games road trip. "The list of contests this season will be much longer than usual, and will include games with the strongest teams of the South. To make a favorable showing, a strong team must be turned out. The material for a strong team is at hand."

Indeed it was. But, as the *Purple* noted, "The main strength of the team is in the men behind the line.... Unless radical improvement takes place Sewanee will be lacking in line positions....The scrub men have been able to make repeated gains through the Varsity line....While the line as a whole is rather weak, the two end positions are causing the most trouble....During the past week several of the best men were injured, which has further complicated the matter."

In an earlier editorial, the *Purple* had appealed for more students to turn out for football practice. "Many men in the various departments of the university and especially in the Medical Department are needed in the football squad. They will find the exercise an agreeable relaxation from the toil of study. Besides they will gain many advantages from a physical point of view."

The precise nature of Sewanee workouts during the summer and into early fall was not described in print, but a fair idea of what took place on Hardee Field can be presumed from a book edited by Walter Camp entitled *How to Play Football.* A chapter by James G. Lathrop discussed training, both pre-season and between games.

Lathrop felt that most coaches tended to overwork their squads and thereby hindered their overall physical condition. He suggested that players so overtrained would enter games too tired to do their best, that practice sessions should be limited so players would be left with "reserve strength." To condition players, he recommended running spurts of 50 yards, interspersed with walking.

Because of the summer months available for practice at Sewanee, chances are that the players, practicing without benefit of a coach, built up their stamina and speed with daily calisthenics and running.

Coach Suter, who had starred in the Ivy League, later credited much of his squad's great season to its physical conditioning. Having benefitted from rigorous training at Princeton, he knew what had to be done at Sewanee. As related in a 1944 interview with Grantland Rice, Suter applied the necessary discipline to the men on the mountain.

As Sewanee approached the '99 season, debate increased, especially in the East, over whether football was too physical and whether road trips were keeping players away from classrooms too much.

On Oct. 13 a *Purple* editor wrote: "We understand there has been more or less discussion—and some adverse criticism—as to the advisability of prolonged football trips in general and our prospective Texas trip in particular. Some people...delight in compiling statistics about the number of recitations the team will miss, in telling how disastrous to all system and organization in classwork a 10-days' absence from the mountain must be, in counting up the number of students we will therefore lose because their dear mamas will not send them to a school where discipline is so lax and holidays given for such trifling foolishness as football, and in stating it to be their incontrovertible opinion that we are going to be beaten anyway, and so, even if there were no other reasons we had better suck our thumbs and stay at home.

"The *Purple* is tolerant and thinks that every man is the owner of his own mind, but we do wish that these 'croakers' would mind their mental ways—a jackdaw is preferable to a raven—and if they can't open their mouths without croaking, pray let them not open them at all....

"Discussion was in order after the motion had been made and seconded—that was sometime ago—but now that it has been passed and has been ratified by the university authorities, and we are going, let us give the team our moral, which is as important as our financial, support. We do not intend to go into a discussion of the healthfulness of college athletics; we assume that to start with. The man that does not believe in athletics can never be convinced that they are anything but a bane to education, and so our words would be wasted.

"Trips are good for the men, trips advertise the university as nothing can, and in our individual case that is what is most needed—and any professor will tell you that it is very much better, from the standpoint of classwork, to take one long trip and play three or four games instead of making a separate trip each time. A 10-day absence is no more demoralizing than one a third as long...."

The *Purple* could have reminded its readers that Sewanee athletes were required to maintain a 2 average (equivalent to B) in grades and their conduct had to be satisfactory to school deans.

Looking ahead to the season opener with Georgia, the *Purple* summed up the pre-season work this way: "Sewanee will have a very light team this year, and from present indications will be rather weak on defense. The linemen will have to settle down to hard work and the backs, tackles and ends must get the interference down better."

Perhaps that writer was taking his cues from a coach trying to build a fire under what already was a strong team. The "weak defense" Suter worried about would hold 11 of 12 opponents scoreless!

So, now it was play ball for '99 with Georgia first up and Georgia Tech to be played only two days later, a double-header of sorts to be played in Atlanta.

Sewanee had played Georgia three times prior to 1899 and had won only one of the three, so the Bulldogs couldn't be taken lightly. In fact, according to *Outing* magazine's account of the game, overconfidence was Georgia's problem.

Faulty play-calling by the Bulldog quarterback gave Sewanee the ball in Georgia territory several times in the first half, and on one of those occasions Seibels went in for a touchdown. In the second half steady running by Seibels, Kilpatrick and Simkins led to a second Sewanee touchdown. Simkins kicked both points-after and Sewanee won 12-0. After a clean game throughout, goodwill overflowed. The defeated Georgians cheered the victors and the purple-clad visitors returned the cheers.

Sewanee stayed over in Atlanta and on Monday walloped Georgia Tech 32-0. Diddy Seibels scored four of his team's six touchdowns and had a 75-yard scoring run called back because of a rules infraction.

The *Purple* noted that, along with the two victories, Sewanee cleared more than one hundred dollars in Atlanta.

Coach Suter expressed himself as well satisfied with the trip and began planning for the University of Tennessee Volunteers, who would be visiting Hardee Field five days later, Oct. 28. That would make three games played within seven days for Sewanee, a warmup for the Texas trip down the road.

Tennessee, whose teams would climb to the top of the football world four decades later, was no match for Sewanee in 1899, losing 46-0 in heavy rain. Seibels had another field day, scoring three touchdowns, Wilson had two and Kilpatrick, Gray and Pearce one each. Simkins kicked six points-after.

Southwestern Presbyterian University of Clarksville proved on Nov. 3 to be another softie. Seibels ran for three more touchdowns as Sewanee romped 54-0.

In preparing for the trip west, Suter's team had won four games and scored 144 points while holding opponents scoreless.

Even so, the upcoming five games in six days, all on the road and against name schools, appeared to be foolhardy at the least, suicidal at the most.

VI

"Don't you remember...?"

H ad Sewanee chartered a second special car, this one for cheerleaders and other supporters, an ardent and vocal crew—the university's dormitory matrons—would have been given the first seats.

Described as the football team's staunchest supporters, the matrons did much more than darn the students' socks and cheer them at home games. Before factory-made equipment became available, they cut out and stitched early Sewanee teams' uniforms, somewhat skimpy outfits of padded pants and jerseys.

The matrons were in the depot crowd that gave the '99 squad a hearty sendoff for the week-long trip, joining in spirited yells such as:

Rah, rah, ree, who are we?

S-e-w-a-n-e-e-, double e!

Rough, tough, we are the stuff,

We play football, never get enough!

During the departure hubbub, an embarrassing oversight occurred: The players' new shoes were left behind at the Sewanee depot. But Manager Luke Lea was a resourceful fellow, not given to wringing his hands. At first opportunity he contacted someone back at Sewanee and asked that the shoes be dispatched on the next train through Cowan, a town nine miles down the mountain from Sewanee and the station where the squad boarded its chartered Pullman.

Fortunately the footwear was properly routed and arrived in Austin before the kickoff of the Texas game.

Perhaps one day a descendant of a '99 player will find a diary in an old trunk in the attic and share day-by-day details of the five-games trip. Until that time information must be gleaned from brief accounts in the *Sewanee*

Purple, from comments in newspaper interviews with players and Coach Suter years after the trip and from letters written by alumni who attended one or more of the five games.

Road trips were nothing new to Sewanee football teams. The point has been made that, because of its isolated mountain campus, Sewanee played most of its games on the road, sometimes two games in three days to keep expenses down. Pullman sleepers provided both a comfortable ride and convenient overnight lodging, along with a place to snack and study. When Luke Lea made reservations for the trip west, he was dealing from experience.

Estimates of the total mileage involved in what was to become known as "the Texas trip" have ranged from 2,000 to 3,000. A researcher trying to pin down an accurate figure got generous help from Charles R. Castner, a retired railroader serving as a consultant in the archives and records center at the University of Louisville.

From copies of the *Travelers' Official Guide of Railways* (1893 and 1910 issues), Castner put together this route of the Sewanee special:

Cowan to Nashville to Memphis on the Nashville, Chattanooga and St. Louis line, 13 hours; Memphis to Texarkana to Austin on the Missouri Pacific (actually, the MP's predecessors, St. Louis & Iron Mountain and International Great Northern), 18 hours; Austin to Houston to New Orleans on the Southern Pacific, 18 hours; New Orleans to Baton Rouge to Memphis on the Illinois Central (actually, the IC's predecessor, Yazoo & Miss. Valley), 15 hours; Memphis to Nashville to Cowan (and Sewanee), 13 hours.

Total mileage on that route came to 2,307. Total hours noted, Castner said, were the elapsed travel time via each railroad. That does not include time spent changing trains and waiting for connections. And not figured in, of course, is time spent for games, side trips, etc.

In any case, counting side trips, the Sewanee squad traveled about 2,500 miles.

The Pullman was a motel on wheels, affording comfortable sleeping berths and daytime seating. By the early 1890s gas lights had become standard on passenger trains, then electric lights became available, so by 1899 the players probably had ample opportunity to study before turning in each evening. One account indicates they got out their textbooks at every opportunity.

What of food and drink? Virtually every article written about the Texas trip mentions the two barrels of Tremlett Spring drinking water that were put aboard the Pullman. That private supply, from the Sewanee mountain spring, was protection against the risks of drinking from a different water supply at every stop.

The players probably took aboard the usual between-meals snacks and had their meals either in dining cars (mentioned in the *Purple*) or at eateries along the way as opportunity afforded.

In the daily reports Lea telegraphed to Sewanee, there was no mention of food. So while available food may not always have been sumptuous, at least it apparently did not affect performance on the playing field. The evening in New Orleans, after the Tulane game, provided opportunity for gourmet dining, and with Luke Lea handling the travel budget, chances are the party took advantage.

Because of Sewanee's academic standards, the players probably spent much of their travel time studying. After all, they soon would be practicing physicians, lawyers, priests and business executives. But according to the *Purple's* recapitulation of the trip, they found time for card games, singing, collegians' customary horseplay, and for taking in the countrysides of five states.

A half-century after the Texas trip, substitute end Ralph Black reminisced in a letter to captain and half-back Diddy Seibels: "Don't you remember our breakfast at Texarkana, where the train stopped for timeout, the stories of the street shootings across the stateline which was down the center of the main street where sheriffs could not cross to make arrests—the fancy calls of the restaurant man—ham and eggs, etc.: keep 'em red eyed, slap 'em once, etc."

When time permitted at wayside stops, the players got out for calisthenics to keep muscles loose and run dummy plays. Such stops also helped break the monotony of the long ride.

The Pullman would be the squad's home most of the

trip, and it served them well. But the long, tiring rides and five tough football games in the next six days appeared to be too much of a challenge, even for a squad in peak condition.

Luke Lea reported back to Sewanee that the players got a good rest Wednesday night prior to Thursday's game with the University of Texas in Austin. The talk around the excited town was that Texas intended to teach Sewanee a lesson.

VII

Thursday, Nov. 10 at Austin: Sewanee 12, Texas 0

H ad the 21 Sewanee football players who arrived in Austin, Tex., the evening of Nov. 8, 1899, been inclined toward entertainment before turning in, opportunities were within walking distance of their hotel.

Firmly established as the state capital, Austin still bore marks of a frontier town where pistol totin' was still in vogue with men and youths, but also where cultural and civic events competed for attention with saloons and gambling dens.

Beer gardens provided relaxation and entertainment for both men and women, and above some saloons games of chance such as poker, monte, chuck-a-luck and keno flourished. And if you knew where to look, drugs were available. Citizen William Sydney Porter, famed later as writer O. Henry, had complained publicly about "opium finds" in the city.

Offsetting the seamy side, Austin was becoming a sports- and recreation-minded city, helped along by the rapidly growing University of Texas. Along with baseball and the still-new game of football, there were rowing regattas on the city's new public lake.

On the night of their arrival Sewanee football players would not have their heads turned by bright lights and frivolity. After arriving on the 7 o'clock train, they went straight to their rooms at the Driskill Hotel, the Austin *Daily Statesman* told its readers the next day. Besides, many of the players had seen something of Austin the year before when Sewanee had come to town and defeated the Longhorns 4-0.

That loss had been the only blot on the Texas record in

1898; in fact, the Sewanee points had been the only ones scored on Texas all season, so the talk around campus and town was that this time Texas would "teach Sewanee to know defeat."

The school that one day would turn out such stars as Bobby Layne, Tommy Nobis and Earl Campbell had begun football only a year or so later than Sewanee and by 1899 was challenging intersectional rivals such as Vanderbilt, LSU and Tulane. The Longhorns already had played and won three games in '99 when Sewanee came to town.

The *Statesman's* game-day headline read "The game promises to be a royal one from start to finish." The story writer noted that the visitors would outweigh the Longhorns about four and a half pounds per man, but that the Texans had been practicing "behind closed gates," had made gratifying progress and expected to win.

Coach Suter listed these Sewanee starters and their weights:

Sims, left end, 154; Jones, left tackle, 175; Keyes, left guard, 190; Poole, center, 184; Claiborne, right guard, 190; Bolling, right tackle, 173; Pearce, right end, 135; Wilson, quarterback, 151; Kilpatrick, left halfback, 165; Seibels, right halfback, 155; Simkins, fullback, 163.

Pearce's listed weight of 135 contrasts with the 114 Suter would remember when being interviewed by Grantland Rice in 1944. In fairness to the coach, he had almost half a century to forget! (Later in the season Pearce was listed at 125, so about the only certainty is that he was small but exceptionally strong.)

Texas' weights ranged from quarterback Russ at 136 to right guard Sams at 220.

The game was a homecoming of sorts for four Texans on the Sewanee squad, especially for Ormond Simkins, whose father taught several years in the University of Texas Law School. The others were Sims, Bolling and Jones.

Fans from as far away as Houston and Dallas traveled to Austin for the game, helping push the crowd to 2,000 or so. The Texas Athletic Council apologized for raising the ticket price to $1, but the council said the price was necessary to raise money for an upcoming Texas road trip. The 1898 Sewanee game in Austin had cost the school $876, which was $203 more than receipts.

Football programs, providing starting lineups and other information, already were part of the college scene. The Texas-Sewanee program included, for first-time fans, this capsule description of football:

"The game of foot ball (sic) is very simple in its outline. It is played by teams of eleven men each. The object of each side is to carry the ball behind the goal line of the opposing team. When one side accomplishes this, it is said to have made a *touch down*, which counts five points and carries with it the privilege of a *try* at kicking point from the 25-yard line of the opposing team. A goal counts one point and consists of sending the ball between the upright posts and above the horizontal bar. Points may be scored in a few other ways, more or less unusual, the most common being by kicking a *goal from field*, which counts five points. The conditions of a *goal from field* are the same as those for a *goal*, save that the position of the ball in reference to the goal is not limited."

The *Statesman* reported that by kickoff time, 3 o'clock, "There was an immense crowd in attendance. They came pouring in from every section of the city and country."

"They were all there," the paper's story added, "highly bedecked in colors. The Varsity colors, as might have been expected, predominated, but the visitors had a number of loyal admirers also who wore their colors with all the proud feeling due the occasion."

Among the visitors was a 14-year-old lad named James N. Young, whose brother had attended Sewanee in 1892 and who had spent a summer there with his mother and two sisters. In a 1954 letter to Ralph Black, a substitute on the '99 team, Young would recall his anticipation of watching the game: "For several days before the big game I could hardly sleep; and I don't think I ate enough to keep a cat alive!....

"Then, too, I well remember Simkins' marvelous punting—his long, beautiful spirals—and line plunging—and the marvelous teamwork of the Sewanee players, who acted as though they had played the game for many years together." Young would be a Purple fan all his life. He graduated with a BA from Harvard in 1911.

Before the trip to Texas, Captain Diddy Seibels had admonished his teammates, "Don't get hurt!" Rules in 1899 did not permit a player to re-enter a game if he had left it for any reason, injury included. Seibels' words came back to haunt him early in the Texas game. As the *Statesman* reported: "There were only two accidents (Editor: injuries) during the game. The most painful one was the injury sustained by Capt. Seibels of the Sewanee team, who had his head badly cut and he bled like a hog. He would not quit the game however."

Indeed, Seibels did not quit. He carried the ball impressively throughout the game and scored both Sewanee touchdowns, one in each half. Simkins, playing before home-state Texans, made several long runs and kept Texas backed up with his effective punting.

A story repeated in newspaper accounts of the trip, but not confirmed by this writer, says that when the Longhorns mounted a scoring threat, a proud Tennessean named Bob "Pop" Atkins stood among Texas fans waving $250 and offering to bet it that Texas not only wouldn't score on *that* drive but also wouldn't score at all. As the story, possibly embellished, goes, Longhorn fans swarmed around Atkins to cover the bet. He eventually left the scene $250 richer, but may have had to share his winnings. Word got out that most of the roll Pop gambled had been invested in advance by Sewanee players.

Accounts in both Sewanee and Austin newspapers described a hard-fought game, free of unsportsmanlike conduct. Texas fans were keenly disappointed at losing to Sewanee a second straight year, but they applauded the Purple's smooth and determined play.

The University of Texas student paper, the *Rambler*, gracefully acknowledged defeat—"we were beaten fairly"— then called for action to make future Longhorn teams more competitive. Among the paper's proposals: Require every student to work at least an hour a day in the gymnasium, but let an hour spent in any varsity sport compensate for that hour; institute football practice in the spring (was this the seed for eventual "spring training"?); encourage more students to go out for football; hire an assistant coach; provide a training table (meals) for Texas athletes. (Editor's note: Texas went undefeated the next year!)

Goodwill reigned during Sewane's visit to Austin. The evening after the game the University of Texas German Club hosted a dance for the winning players, but the honorees couldn't dance until the usual wee hours; an overnight train ride to Houston and a game the next afternoon with Texas A&M awaited the Iron-Men-in-the-making.

Immediately after the Texas game, Luke Lea dispatched this telegram: "To Sewanee Purple: Sewanee 12, Texas nothing. Seibels and Simkins, and all the men, played great ball. Crowd not specially large. Features: Sewanee's superb defense on her third-yard line and first down. Game played in Texas territory. Men in good fix."

In its next issue the *Purple* printed the following account of the game:

We have met the enemy and they are ours.

After a tiresome journey of forty-eight hours, in a country where there is a marked difference in the temperature, and on a field surrounded by thousands of our opponents' followers, Sewanee for the second time has shown her superiority over Texas.

That the victory was a well-earned one the detailed score will show. True, the game was principally played in the enemy's territory, but the Texans put up a hard fight, and it was only the indomitable, indefinable Sewanee spirit that carried the ball over for the two touchdowns and a victory.

The Varsity played its usual faultless game, and, as Manager Lea's telegram states, the feature of the game was Sewanee's superb defense on her three-yard line, when Texas had the ball, and three downs in which to cross the goal line. Thrice did Texas hurl her backs against the purple wall, and thrice did Sewanee repel the onslaughts. Then the whistle blew on the third down, and Texas had lost her one opportunity of scoring.

The Purple *is indebted to Mr. W.B. Thompson for a detailed account of the game and a full description as follows:*

The lineup:

Sewanee—Pearce, right end; Bolling, right tackle; Claiborne, right guard; Poole, center; Keyes, left guard; Jones, left tackle; Sims, left end; Wilson, quarterback; Seibels (Capt.), right halfback; Gray, left halfback; Simkins, fullback. (Editor's note: That lineup meant either that Suter changed his mind and started Gray instead of Kilpatrick at left half, or that Kilpatrick had either been injured in practice or become ill. He was back as a starter the next day against Texas A&M.)

Texas—Schreiner, right end; McMahon, right tackle; Sams, right guard; Overshiner, center; Scott, left guard; Hart (Capt.), left tackle; Monteith, left end; Russ, quarterback; Bethea, right half-back; Keller, left halfback; Cole, fullback.

Sewanee wins toss and takes goal, with wind in her favor. Keller kicks off 35 yards, Pearce brings ball back 15. Seibels tries left end; no gain. Seibels tries right tackle; no gain. Simkins punts 40 yards. Keller downed in his tracks. Russ fumbles and loses 5 yards, Keller punts 20. Seibels runs back 10. Sewanee's ball.

Simkins bucks center; no gain. Gray runs around right end 10 yards, Simkins bucks 6 yards. Seibels around right end 5 yards. Wilson no gain. Gray no gain, and Seibels gets 3 yards around right tackle, but loses ball. Texas' ball. Bethea gets 10 yards around left end. Cole bucks center; no gain. Keller kicks 40 yards, Simkins runs back 20. Sewanee's ball.

Seibels goes through right tackle for 40 yards. Simkins hits center for 10 yards. Simkins hits center 1 yard. Seibels gets through right tackle 4 yards, and is slightly hurt. Simkins bucks for 4 yards. Seibels gets 3 yards outside tackle. Ball goes to Texas on a fumble. Keller hits left tackle for 10 yards. Texas gets 15 yards on an offside play. Cole bucks for 4 yards, Keller punts 35 yards. Seibels returns ball 5. Sewanee's ball. Gray tries left end 3 yards, Simkins gets 10 yards through the line. Ball goes over on technicality.

Texas fumbles, Pearce falls on the ball. Seibels gets 2 yards by right end. Wilson fails to gain. Ball goes over on Texas' 35-yard line. Bethea gets 25 yards around the end, Keller gets 3 yards. Bethea bucks the line for 5 yards. Sewanee's ball on technicality. Sewanee gets 15 yards by offside play. Simkins gets through the line for 35 yards. Seibels tries left tackle but fails to gain. Ball on Texas' 15-yard line. Gray gets 2 yards, Simkins gets 1. 7 yards to goal line. Seibels hits line for touchdown. Pearce kicks goal. Nine minutes to play. Score, Sewanee 6, Texas 0.

Keller kicks 40 yards and Gray runs back 15. Seibels gets 35 yards around end. Seibels hits left without gain. Simkins fails to gain. Sewanee's ball on Texas' 45-yard line. Gray gets 1 yard through right tackle. Seibels tries left end with no gain. Simkins hits line; no gain. Simkins punts 40 yards. Russ returns ball 15 yards. Keller gets 30 yards by left end. Russ gets 5 through line.

Bethea fails to gain. Keller kicks 30 yards. Sewanee's ball on Texas' 45-yard line.

Seibels gets 3 yards. Sewanee fumbles, but falls on ball, losing 10 yards. Seibels gets 20 yards through line. Simkins gets 20 yards through line. Simkins gets 10 yards through tackle. Simkins tries center without gain (Editor: Yardage miscalculated).

Time called, with Sewanee's ball on Texas' 35-yard line. Score, Sewanee 6, Texas 0.

Second half

Simkins kicks 30 yards. Russ runs ball back 15. Schreiner gets 5 yards by right end. Bethea gets 4 yards. Keller gets 5 on left end. Cole bucks center for 1 yard. Keller kicks for 35 yards. Seibels runs ball back for 10 yards. Simkins kicks 35 yards. Texas' ball on 45-yard line.

Cole bucks for 1 yard. Bethea tries right end, but fails to gain. Keller punts 40 yards, Seibels comes back 15. Simkins kicks 35 yards, Russ runs ball back 10 and is hurt. Texas' ball. Cole bucks for 3 yards. Cole gets 3 yards by tackle. First down. Schreiner gets 7 yards by right end. Keller gains 5 yards by left end. Bethea gains 5 yards past tackle. Texas fumbles, but secures ball. Keller punts 40 yards, and Seibels gets a fair catch on the 20-yard line. Simkins punts 35 yards. Keller gets 55 yards through line (Editor's note: The "55" may have been a typographical error; perhaps should have been 5). Schreiner gains 5 yards outside tackle. Cole hits left tackle for no gain.

Sewanee gets ball. Simkins kicks 40 yards. Russ runs back 35 yards and goes out of game. Bethea gets 3 yards through left side of line, and repeats it on right side. Keller gets 2 yards on end. Half a foot to gain. Bethea bucks center for 45 yards. Schreiner gets 7 yards outside tackle. Keller gains 3 yards in same place. Bethea gets 3 yards through left tackle.

Texas' ball, first down, on Sewanee's 30-yard line. Cole bucks center for 3 yards. Bethea fails to gain through center. Schreiner gets 5 yards through right tackle. Monteith gets 3 yards. Bethea bucks left tackle for 2 yards. Cole bucks for 5 yards. Bethea hits left tackle for no gain. Schreiner gets 2 yards outside right tackle. Ball on Sewanee's 8-yard line. Texas loses ball on downs.

Seibels gets 5 yards through tackle. Gray gets 5 yards outside tackle, and then 5 yards through line. Simkins bucks for 4 yards. Seibels gets 3 yards outside tackle, and Gray gets 10 yards *through tackle. Seibels gets 5 yards, Simkins 4 yards, Gray 7 yards, Gray 3 yards. Seibels gains 10 yards on tackle. Ball on Texas' 35-yard line.*

Sewanee fumbles but falls on the ball. Gray gets 6 yards on mass play, and repeats it for 8 yards. Seibels fails; no gain. Gray gains 3 yards by mass play. Ball in 18 yards of Texas' goal. Seibels no gain, Gray no gain.

Simkins bucks, and Keller gets ball. Keller gains outside tackle 2 yards. Monteith gets 4 yards past left end. McMahon gains 1 yard. Sewanee gets the ball. Seibels bucks to Texas' 19-yard line. Gray gets 2 yards through right tackle. Simkins bucks for 12 yards. Ball on Texas' 9-yard line. Simkins bucks again, but fails. Seibels bucks for 9 yards and a touchdown. Pearce kicks goal. Score, Sewanee 12, Texas 0.

Two minutes and 45 seconds to play. Keller kicks 45 yards, Simkins runs back 15. Texas gets the ball on Sewanee's 35-yard line. Keller bucks left end for a gain. Schreiner gets 5 yards on right. Keller gains 3 yards. Texas fumbles and Bethea falls on the ball. Forty-five seconds to play. Ball on Sewanee's 25-yard line. Keller tries placekick for a goal, but fails. The whistle blows.

Seibels, Simkins, Gray, Claiborne and Bolling did the best work for Sewanee.

VIII

Friday, Nov. 11 at Houston: Sewanee 10, Texas A&M 0

Motorists zipping along Houston's Interstate 610 loop in the 1990s, seeing the skyscrapers downtown and in the Galleria, the Astrodome, the medical center and other attractions, might have trouble envisioning the Houston the Sewanee football players saw on the 1899 Friday morning they arrived to play Texas A&M.

In Sam Houston's namesake city, Coach Billy Suter's players could see horsedrawn vehicles and pedestrians sharing downtown streets with trolley cars. Many Houston housewives were still doing their grocery shopping at Market Square, and as a historian later would note, horses stood at curbside while their owners did business in nearby financial establishments.

Even before the War Between the States a Texas newspaper boasted that Houston "had become the focus of immigration from all directions and center of most of the spirit and enterprise of Texas." A year after Sewanee came to town the nosecount of citizens was 44,633. Just under a century later it was nearing 2 million.

A Houston brag point in 1899 was City Auditorium, which had been built in 1895 at Main and McGowan to host the national reunion of Confederate veterans. By the time Sewanee arrived, the city was providing a wide variety of entertainment and recreation for residents and visitors. One entertainment that Houston wanted more of in 1899 was the still-new game of college football, and nearby A&M at Bryan appeared an attractive way to fill the need.

The Sewanee team that had played in Austin the day before and traveled overnight to Houston would play

A&M that afternoon and soon afterward entrain for New Orleans. The players had no time to take in the sights in Houston.

A&M had made a tentative start with football in 1894, for some reason had laid off the game in 1895, then returned to it in '96 and by '98 played a schedule of six games.

When Luke Lea arranged for Sewanee to play A&M, filling the last gap on that five-games-in-six-days lineup, Houston agreed to be host. A&M would benefit from the big-city exposure and Sewanee could conveniently pause there for a game between its Austin and New Orleans stops.

Sewanee's only starting lineup change from the Texas game was at left halfback, where Rex Kilpatrick would replace Charles Quintard Gray.

The *Houston Daily Post*, loyal to the Aggies and encouraging them to make Houston their football home, reported that A&M put up a better fight against Sewanee than had Varsity (Texas) the day before. The *Post* reporter wrote that "the Sewanee men who would discuss it said they considered A&M had played a much better game than Varsity did Thursday."

The daily's game account seems to support that. Sewanee scored its two touchdowns as time was about to run out in each half, Simkins scoring the first, Wilson the second, as Sewane won 10-0. Both extra-point attempts were missed.

Attendance was not as large as expected, the *Post* reported without giving a specific figure, but the crowd was enthusiastic and "Sewanee was not without friends."

"The Purple was worn by many and a compliment to Tennessee visitors was the wearing of their colors by some of the prettiest girls of the Lone Star state. One young lady actually went to an expense of 54 cents for purple ribbon and she would not part with an inch of it."

Football historians occasionally have sought to determine when megaphones were first used by cheerleaders. The *Post* game account included this paragraph: "The cadets used a number of megaphones during the game to shout applause to their fellows on the gridiron."

The starting lineups as published in the *Post*:

een of the 21 Sewanee Iron
who won five games in six
ays posed with Coach Billy
uter (back row, in baseball
and Manager Luke Lea (on
Suter's right, wearing hat).
nt row, left to right: Bunny
rce, end; Charles Quintard
Gray, substitute halfback;
ddy Seibels, right halfback
d captain; Warbler Wilson,
terback, and Bartlet Sims,
end. Middle row: Richard
ing, tackle; Rex Kilpatrick,
left halfback; W. H. Poole,
; H. S. Keyes, guard; John
W. Jones, tackle; Ormond
nkins, fullback. Back row:
Ralph P. Black, substitute;
illiam S. Claiborne, guard;
; Suter; J. L. Kirby-Smith,
substitute; Dan Hull,
substitute.

ddy Seibels, right halfback
and captain

Time out for a studio visit: Coach
Suter (left) with quarterback
Warbler Wilson

Fullback Ormond Simkins,
whom Seibels called the team's
best player

ee captain Diddy Seibels was inducted into the Alabama Sports Hall of
n 1992. Viewing the Seibels plaque: Sons Henry G. "Buzz" Seibels, Jr.,
) and Kelly Seibels (right) with cousin and former Birmingham Mayor
Seibels.

William Claiborne,
guard

W. H. Poole, center

Bunny Pea

Diddy Seibels as
business executive

Harris Cope (left),
'99 Iron Men
substitute and later
Sewanee head
coach, as Howard
College coach in the
1920s.

Halfback Rex Kilpatrick, who kicked the winning field goal against North Carolina

Ormond Simkins, in an *Outing* magazine photo when he was chosen All-Southern after the '99 season. Seibels and Poole also made All-Southern.

Meanwhile, back at a Sewanee studio: Kilpatrick (front), Wilso (right) and Black.

Guard William Claiborne, who had lost an eye, tried out a protective patch. Whether he wore the patch in game action could not be determined.

Iron Men quarterback and 1900 captain
Warbler Wilson at a family gathering many
years later with Mrs. Wilson and grandson
William B. "Blackie" Wilson III

n Men substitute Dan Hull,
o became a boxing
moter in Savannah, Ga.

Sub Iron Men end Ralph
Black, for many years a
professor of engineering at
Georgia Tech

Rare photograph of 1900 field goal attempt, apparently by Rex Kilpatrick
had kicked a goal in '99 to defeat North Carolina.

THE UNIVERSITY OF THE SOUTH
PLAYED AND WON **5** FOOTBALL GAME
FROM **5** DIFFERENT TEAMS IN **6** DAYS
THEIR GOAL LINE WAS *NOT* CROSS.

This salute to Sewanee's Iron Men was illustrated in John Hix's newspap
panel "Strange As It Seems" in the 1930s.

Sewanee—Sims, left end; Jones, left tackle; Keyes, left guard; Poole, center; Claiborne, right guard; Bolling, right tackle; Pearce, right end; Wilson, quarterback; Seibels (C), right halfback; Kilpatrick, left halfback; Simkins, fullback.

A&M—Schultz, left end; Moseley (C), left tackle; Kildow, left guard; Boettcher, center; Weinert, right guard; Astin, right tackle; Prather, right end; Simpson, quarterback; Johnson, right halfback; Fahring, left halfback; Japhet, fullback.

Referee, Killorin of Georgia; umpire, Blacklock; time-keepers, Nicholson (U. of La.) for Sewanee; Prof. South for A&M; linemen, Hull for Sewanee, Burke for A&M.

Following is the game account that ran in the *Post* (Editor's note: The A and M abbreviation was the paper's style back then):

A. and M. won the toss and chose the south goal. The first play developed the fact that Sewanee had a lot of work cut out to win. There was no perceptible advantage for either team until A. and M. got hold of the ball after some minutes of play: the Cadets went through the center and gained five yards.

Brown punted to Sewanee's 15-yard line, but the umpire sent the ball back, declaring it an offside play. Brown punted but the ball was cleverly returned. Brown again punted but Sewanee sent it back again.

A. and M.'s ball and they made an advance through center, but Sewanee finally lined up and held them. Sewanee developed its game and tried around the ends, gaining twenty yards, but A. and M. stopped them at the 30-yard line and sent the ball back into Sewanee ground.

Every time Sewanee tried center they failed, but around the ends they went easily. Jones finally got the ball and made a long run to the A. and M. 5-yard line (Editor's note: The rules then permitted linemen to carry the ball). Sewanee was playing hard and by sheer weight carried the ball to within a foot of the goal line and despite every effort of the cadets, Simkins made the touchdown. Pearce tried for goal and missed.

The rest of the half was without gain for either, though Wilson made a long run and A. and M. punted twice, but the kicks were too light. Score 5 to 0 for Sewanee.

Second half

In the second half Sewanee had both sun and wind back of them. Sewanee started in for blood and had the ball on the A. and M. 25-yard line. They again lost ground in trying to go through the center and the scrimmage was a tough one.

A. and M. got the ball and went through all right for fifteen yards but on attempt to go around (end) they lost it.

After they again got the ball Astin bucked the center and made a slight gain. Ball was snapped to Fahring who made a 20-yard run around the end. Astin again took it through the center.

Then Sewanee got the ball and for the first time they made progress through A. and M.'s center. Kilpatrick was shoved through and on every move gained ground—5, 1, 7, 3 yards. Wilson was given the ball and around the right end he went carrying the ball to the A. and M. 5-yard line. He would possibly have gone to a touchdown had not a buggy been driven into such a position that he could not avoid a collision. A moment after, however, he got around the left end and made the touchdown.

Pearce kicked and again missed goal. Score: Sewanee 10, A. and M. 0.

As noted earlier, because football was still in its pioneer years, so was football reporting. Thus, hometown newspapers printed home-flavored accounts, but all things considered, the following report of Sewanee's triumph over A&M, published in the Aggie campus paper *The Battalion*, seems a reasonably accurate summary. In two differences in the lineups, the *Battalion* had Dwyer at left half and Brown at fullback.

A. and M. went down in honorable defeat before the mighty Sewanee team in what proved to be one of the fiercest and most brilliant contests ever seen on the southern gridiron.

The game was played in Houston on Nov. 10 and witnessed by a crowd of about 600 people, who made up in enthusiasm what they lacked in numbers. Sewanee has a team of gentlemanly players who go into the game for all there is in it and play a hard, fast and beautiful game of football. They are unmistakably the champions of the South this year, and the A. and M. cannot but feel gratified that she gave Sewanee her hardest and fiercest battle of the year, resulting in the lowest score.

Sewanee had every advantage over the Cadets—in age, weight and experience—having been carefully coached for the last four or five years in the same style of play, while on the Cadet side the team was composed of material untried and inexperienced, who had been coached to play an entirely new system of football.

Yet, with only six weeks of practice they gave the champions such a run for their money as they never had before. It was the first time the Cadets had ever met a team from beyond the borders of Texas. They went into the fight with no premonitions of disaster. They were there to convince their neighbors that they knew some football.

And yet, another thing, there was the Varsity score with Sewanee to better and force Varsity to admit them as her rivals and give them a game for the championship of Texas. With these incentives they fought with the obstinate courage of true Texans.

As in Varsity game the A. and M. line stood like a wall of adamant and only once in the latter part of first half was Sewanee able to pierce it for any substantial gains, while the A. and M. backs and forwards plunged through the Sewanee line for large gains at almost every attempt. Astin's work in this respect was particularly brilliant. The way this human catapult tore through the Sewanee line was a sight to gladden one's heart—unless it was a Sewanee heart.

Sewanee's best gains were made around the A. and M.'s right end, yet she did not get away for any hair-raising runs, for there were always several A. and M. tacklers after the ball who downed the runner before he had gone very far.

Nevertheless the game was replete with brilliant plays, short dodging, dashes, terrific tackles, beautiful line bucking and irresistible mass plays, together with an occasional fumble and the reckless attempts to recover the ball, kept the excitement to the highest pitch and contributed ever to the delirious uncertainty as to the result.

A. and M. won the choice of goals and chose south goal, with wind and sun at her back. Sewanee kicked off. The first play developed the fact that Sewanee had much work before her. The manner in which the Cadets ripped up her line and plunged through for gains made her defense look like the proverbial "thirty cents."

Down the field went A. and M. with the ball strewing the path with Purple wreckage, and it looked like a score when A. and M. got ball on Sewanee's 15 yard line, but umpire called ball back to mid-field for off-side play and the A. and M. visions of a touchdown went glimmering.

Only once afterwards did they get near enough to score, but an error in judgment prevented a goal from place kick, with almost certain results.

Brown's atrocious fumbling of Sewanee's long punts made it possible for her to get near enough to the A. and M. goal line to score and win the game. Sewanee got ball on such fumble in A. and M. territory, by a neat end run, carried it to A. and M.'s 8 yard line. Here the Cadets made a heroic stand, but Sewanee's superior weight forced them back inch by inch until within a foot of the line.

Here with a din and a wriggle in a last desperate effort Simkins was shoved over the coveted goal line for a touchdown. Pearce missed goal.

The minute and a half left to play in the first half was without gain for either side.

The second half was a repetition of the first, with Sewanee getting around Prather's end with greater freedom and, also for a long gain, past Schultz, on a quarter-back trick play, which brought ball to A. and M.'s 5 yard line. On a similar play around Prather's end the touchdown was scored with but five seconds left to play.

Pearce missed the goal and the game ended with score of 10 to 0 in favor of Sewanee.

Sewanee earned her game by playing hard, fast, clean, aggressive football, when Brown's deplorable fumbles gave her the ball, through the sharp work of her ends, within striking distance of the A. and M. goal line. To those who witnessed the game it was evident that the game would have ended with a zip-zip score had not A. and M. fumbled in such a costly manner the Sewanee punts.

However, as marriage is the only thing more uncertain than a football game, there are several critical occasions all plastered over with "what might have beens" if—yes, if—but that has no effect on history already made.

IX

Saturday, Nov. 12 at New Orleans: Sewanee 23, Tulane 0

Billy Suter must have been elated with his team's performances against Texas and Texas A&M.

Of any concerns he may have felt as the party left Sewanee, player condition and stamina were not among them. Sewanee's customary several weeks' practice jump on all opponents would weigh heavily in Purple favor all season long. If that advantage could be translated into points, the two-touchdown margins over both the Longhorns and Aggies probably could be attributed to superb physical condition and fine-tuned play execution.

Capt. Diddy Seibels' severe forehead cut was the only major injury suffered thus far and, although Seibels probably wanted to continue playing, Suter apparently convinced him he should stay out of the Tulane game and give the wound a chance to begin healing.

Even in the early years of football, coaches had to fret about mental letdowns, and the 350-mile overnight ride from Houston to New Orleans was opportunity for Suter to mull over that concern. After all, ahead were fun-loving New Orleans and a Tulane team hungry for victory in its first 1899 game.

Five years earlier when Tulane, striving to improve its football program, was preparing to play Sewanee for the first time, the campus paper, *College Spirit*, had made this appeal: "We cannot impress too strongly upon the men the importance of the Sewanee game." Tulane had lost that one 12-6 and now there was a chance for revenge.

If Suter could have foreseen what Tulane would do a year later—go undefeated and unscored on—he probably would have had a sleepless ride to New Orleans. But

1899 was not to be a Tulane year.

The independent school that philanthropist Paul Tulane had made possible for New Orleans opened in 1884. Because its home city was fun-loving and sports-minded, Tulane caught the sports bug early, and when football caught on in the South in the early 1890s, Tulane wanted in on the act.

In his book *The Rise of Sports in New Orleans 1850-1900*, Dave A. Somers wrote that "people in all ranks of society sought recreation in amusements of every description, including theaters, dances, concerts, opera, Mardi Gras, gambling parlors, and saloons. None of these pastimes claimed a larger following than did organized sports. Thousands of residents joined athletic teams and clubs, hundreds traveled to other cities for competition, and tens of thousands attended athletic events as spectators."

By the turn of the century, Somers reported, New Orleans had better streets, improved lighting, and an urban transit system that let residents live farther from their jobs and, of course, attend sporting events.

Among the sports offerings were horse racing, boxing (prize fighting, it was called then), baseball, tennis, golf, cycling, billiards and football.

City athletic clubs fielded football teams in the game's early years, but gradually college teams attracted more attention. For New Orleans, that meant Tulane; with a growing population to draw from, potential was there for the Green Wave.

Despite campus enthusiasm, however, Tulane's football efforts sputtered, almost stopped, then sputtered again. The school fielded a team in 1893 that managed to defeat upstate LSU 34-0 but lost its other two games, played four tough but losing games in 1894, then finally had a winning season (4-2) in 1895.

Although the first Tulane coach was on the scene in 1896, the Green Wave was only .500 in four games, and in 1897 the school was forbidden by the Southern Intercollegiate Athletic Association to field a team because of a dispute over the eligibility of a player the previous year.

In 1898 John Lombard, who had played on the first

Tulane team, coached the squad as part of his duties as physical education director. In its only games the Wave defeated Mississippi and lost to LSU. Lombard returned as coach in 1899 and prepared to play a Sewanee team victorious the previous two days in Texas. Tulane not only wouldn't score against Sewanee, but also would go without a point in its six other games.

A pre-game newspaper account in New Orleans noted that, perhaps surprisingly, Tulane would have a slight weight advantage, but that Sewanee players were in "the very best physical condition" and despite the two tough games in Texas and the overnight train ride from Houston "can stand this constant tax upon their strength."

An advertisement reminded the public that the game would be played on the Tulane field, that admission was 50 cents and the kickoff would be at 3:30.

The starting lineups, with Gray substituting for Seibels, and the following game report appeared in the *Sewanee Purple*. Actually Gray played left halfback and Kilpatrick moved to right half.

Sewanee—Sims, left end; Jones, left tackle; Keyes, left guard; Poole, center; Claiborne, right guard; Bolling, right tackle; Pearce, right end; Wilson, quarterback; Kilpatrick, right halfback; Gray, left halfback; Simkins, fullback.

Tulane—Kilpatrick, left end; Fitzpatrick, left tackle; Fulton, left guard; Mangum, center; Wilson, right guard; Stearns, right tackle; McGehee, right end; Post, quarterback; Owens, right halfback; Levert, left halfback; Eshleman, fullback.

Sewanee added another victory to her matchless record on Saturday, when she defeated Tulane 23-0. This makes the seventh game that the Varsity have won, and opponents have yet to cross our goal line. The New Orleans Picayune, of Sunday, Nov. 12, had this to say of Sewanee:

"The Tennessee team are (sic) playing a pretty game, potent in defense and attack, and have the line which is often compared to a brick wall, and have the backs, especially the fullback. This player of their team is possibly the star of the eleven. The big fellows in purple, although well-trained and experienced men, accomplished more than an ordinary victory in defeating Tulane. They have been traveling hard for a week. On Thursday they met a very stubborn rival at Austin, Texas, in the University of that

state, and Friday they played at Houston with a team which, judging from the score, was even stronger than the Austin men.

"They traveled all Friday night to keep their engagement with Tulane, and came into the city tired and out of sorts, as athletes will become on railroad journeys. Without much rest they went again on the field, and again scored a victory."

The game in detail:

Sewanee took the kickoff, and Kilpatrick sent the ball 45 yards. Owens gained 5 yards around left end, and Levert failed to gain. Eshleman punted 30 yards, and Simkins ran the ball back 15. Kilpatrick gets 1 yard around left end and adds 3 more on tackle. Gray goes his length through tackle, and Kilpatrick on three plays gets 15 yards.

Wilson springs around end for 10 yards, and Gray drops the ball after being downed. The referee decided that the whistle blew before the ball was lost, however, and Kilpatrick goes the remaining distance for a touchdown. Pearce kicks goal. Time, 6 minutes.

Eshleman kicks off 45 yards, and Kilpatrick returns 10. Simkins punted 35 yards. Post was downed in his tracks. Levert no gain. Owens 10 yards. Owens 5 yards, Levert 20 yards. Sewanee braced up at this juncture and got the ball on downs.

Kilpatrick goes through right tackle for 10 yards, Gray gets 5 yards around right end, Kilpatrick adds 3 more outside of tackle, and Gray plunges through left tackle for 10. Gray then goes 10 yards for the second touchdown. Pearce kicks goal.

Eshleman kicks off 40 yards and Simkins gains 25 before he is stopped. Wilson gets 2 yards. Jones fails to gain. Gray gets 2 yards on a tackle play, and Kilpatrick duplicates same. Gray gets 7 yards on three plays, and Kilpatrick plunges through center for 5 yards. Sewanee then fumbles on Tulane's 10-yard line.

On a fake kick Levert loses 2 yards and fails to gain around right end. Eshleman then punts 30 yards. Sewanee then works the ball down the field by rushes and end runs, and Gray is pushed over for the third touchdown. Pearce misses goal. Time, 23 minutes.

Eshleman kicks off 30 yards, and Simkins advances half that distance before he is downed. Gray gets 3 yards around tackle and Jones is stopped after a gain of 25 yards.

Wilson circles right end for 15 yards and Simkins goes through center for 3 yards. Time is then called, with the ball on Tulane's 20-yard line in Sewanee's possession. Score, Sewanee 17, Tulane 0.

Second half

Eshleman kicks off 35 yards, and Pearce ran the ball up 10. Kilpatrick gets 4 yards through tackle and Simkins punts 45 yards. Levert then makes a pretty run of 20 yards and adds 4 more through tackle.

Eshleman punts 40 yards, and Simkins runs back 20, but drops the ball when tackled. Tulane tries three plays unsuccessfully, and the ball goes over.

Gray is hurt on the next play, and Hull goes in. Jones then circles right end, passes two tacklers, is stopped with a gain of 30 yards. Simkins bucks center for 5 yards. Eshleman is hurt, and Westfeldt replaces him. Kilpatrick then goes 5 yards for the fourth touchdown. Pearce kicks goal. Time, 10 minutes.

The remainder of the game was played in Tulane's territory, and darkness finally set in and time was called. Black replaced Pearce and Brooks relieved Simkins before the end of the second half. Final score, Sewanee 23, Tulane 0.

X

Monday, Nov. 14 at Baton Rouge: Sewanee 34, LSU 0

The Saturday evening after defeating Tulane, Coach Suter and his squad could relax for the first time after arriving in Austin three days before. They would have Sunday off, although had customs of the time permitted, Manager Luke Lea might well have had them playing a Sunday game.

Saturday night in fun-city New Orleans beckoned, but Suter and Lea weren't likely to turn 21 football players loose on the town. With three opponents defeated and two more ahead, sports history was being written.

The limited information available about the trip doesn't suggest which restaurant Lea chose (surely he chose!), but later the players attended a play popular at the time, *Rupert of Hentzau.*

According to the Oct. 16, 1961 issue of *Sports Illustrated*, in the final act "as the dead hero lay in state, Queen Flavia came on stage dressed in mourning clothes of purple velvet." At the sight of their team color, the Sewanee players "burst into a whooping rendition of the Sewanee yell, mystifying actors and audience alike."

With no game scheduled the next day, the players probably had the best sleep of their trip, whether they were in a hotel or their Pullman. Next morning, one account reported, the players went to church, then in the afternoon toured a sugar plantation west of New Orleans. The owner/host was Sewanee alumnus John Dalton Shaffer.

Mercifully for the travel-weary squad the next game stop was less than 100 railroad miles away at upstate Baton Rouge.

Louisiana's capital city for half a century when Sewanee came to town, Baton Rouge then was a big country town still recovering from the 1893 depression. City leaders could boast of 58 retail grocers doing business there, but perhaps an even brighter sign of prosperity had been establishment of a Coca-Cola company, a branch from headquarters in Atlanta.

Photographs of downtown Baton Rouge at century's end don't suggest that the Sewanee visitors spent much time sightseeing, except possibly at boat traffic on the Mississippi River and the Fort Sumter Saloon with a leftover Civil War cannon at its front.

Founded in 1845, Louisiana State took up football in 1893 with a former Johns Hopkins player, C. E. Coates, as coach and a one-game season, a 34-0 drubbing by Tulane. After that inauspicious start, LSU did not have another losing season until the year Sewanee came to town.

The Tigers, as they would become known, opened the '99 season with an 11-0 loss to Mississippi at Meridian but still hoped for a good season. According to the local press, they weren't awed by the visiting Tennesseans' winning streak, but they should have been.

Baton Rouge's *Daily Advocate* said of the LSU-Sewanee meeting: "This is by far the most promising game ever played here, and we fully expect to see two thousand people (conservative estimate) on the grounds that day. The game will be played on an ideal spot on the college grounds and we are sure our boys will reflect great credit upon themselves upon this auspicious occasion."

Since the opening-game defeat by Mississippi, "the boys have secured a number of reenforcements, and among these reenforcements, a number of heavy athletes."

A game account that ran in the LSU campus paper, the *Reveille*, noted that LSU used four substitutes in the first half and three in the second half, and that Sewanee "played four or five substitutes after the first two touchdowns."

Discrepancies in the *Reveille* and the *Sewanee Purple* on identification of ball carriers and yardage gained on particular plays probably resulted, as in other games, from reporters' unfamiliarity with players on the opposing side, from having to cover action from either crowded grandstands or the sidelines, and from unnumbered yard lines. The reporters' biggest help likely came from first-down signals (gaining five yards or more on three downs or fewer) and from signals of touchdowns or goals.

Starting lineups printed in the Memphis *Commercial-Appeal*, reporting the game because Sewanee would be in Memphis the next day to play Mississippi, showed that Sewanee stayed with its regulars. Apparently in trying to correct a typographical error, the paper had Kilpatrick listed as the starter at both left and right halfback, but the game account confirms that Seibels was back in action after sitting out the Tulane game. Simkins was listed as starting at fullback, but may have played little, presumably because of a leg injury.

The lineups:

Sewanee—Sims, left end; Jones, left tackle; Keyes, left guard; Poole, center; Claiborne, right guard; Bolling, right tackle; Pearce, right end; Wilson, quarterback; Kilpatrick, left halfback; Seibels, right halfback; Simkins, fullback.

LSU—Gorham, left end; Aly, left tackle; Laurant, left guard; Chevanne, center; Pratt, right guard; Huyck, right tackle; Laurason, right end; Wall, quarterback; Gremillion, left halfback; Jones, right halfback; Landry, fullback.

Timekeepers were Prof. Atkinson of L.S.U. and Mr. Lea of Sewanee. Referee was Robertson of L.S.U. and umpire was Kaufman of S.A.C. Linesmen were LeSeur of L.S.U. and Hull of Sewanee.

Following is the game account from the *Purple*:

Sewanee won from Louisiana State with ease on Monday of last week. The game was played in Baton Rouge on the college campus and was witnessed by a fair-sized crowd.

Sewanee outplayed the Baton Rouge men at every point, and during the game a number of substitutes were used in Sewanee's makeup.

As usual, Sewanee lost the toss, then started in to play a very aggressive game, as the team was in very good spirits after their rest over Sunday.

After several exchanges of punts, Sewanee carried the ball 60 yards in five plays, Seibels scoring a touchdown, Pearce kicking the goal.

The next kickoff was run back some distance by Sewanee, and then, on the first play, Seibels sprinted 70 yards for a touchdown.

The remainder of the first half was a succession of rapid gains by Gray and Seibels. Near the end of the first half Kilpatrick changed from fullback to left half, Hull took Seibels' place at right half, Brooks taking fullback. The first half ended 17-0. (Editor's note: The Purple account thus omitted a touchdown. The Reveille said "the left halfback circles right end for a touchdown." That would have been Kilpatrick, who had moved to that position. Sims kicked goal for the 17-0 halftime score.)

During the second half more strong playing was seen, Kilpatrick doing some of the finest plunging of the year. Hull also did some very good gaining, while Brooks hit the center hard at times.

Parker was given a chance at halfback, Kirby-Smith at right tackle, and Black on right end, all doing very creditable work.

The second half continued like the first, as a series of end runs and plunges through the line that netted 17 points, a total of 34 for the two halves of 25 and 20 minutes.

The Baton Rouge men played a clean, lively game, the ends tackling well, but Sewanee's defense was so effective that they were unable to advance the ball.

Sewanee was accorded most courteous treatment, and the men enjoyed playing on an almost perfect gridiron.

(Editor's note: Of the three second-half touchdowns, Kilpatrick was credited with one and kicked two goals-after. None of the three accounts—*Reveille*, *Purple*, *Commercial-Appeal*, reported who scored the other two touchdowns in the 34-0 victory.)

XI

Tuesday, Nov. 15 at Memphis: Sewanee 12, Ole Miss 0

When the Sewanee football special reached Memphis, technically the players were back in home country after traveling through Arkansas, Texas, Louisiana and Mississippi. But Memphis was more home turf for the Mississippi Rebels from nearby Oxford, Miss., than for the Middle Tennesseans.

Just as University of Alabama teams always have had a second home in Birmingham, Auburn in Montgomery and Mississippi State in Jackson, Ole Miss has been almost as much at home in Memphis as in Oxford.

The Rebels, as they would become known, hit the ground winning in 1893. In their first season they won four games of five and had had only one losing season before their 1899 meeting with Sewanee. Like most early teams they had changed coaches frequently; in '99 W.H. Lyon of Yale was trying his hand at Oxford.

Arriving Tuesday morning from Baton Rouge, the Sewanee squad had time for sight-seeing before heading for the game field. The *Commercial-Appeal's* pre-game story reminded readers the game would be played at Billings Park that afternoon between the "victorious Sewanee eleven and the long-haired knights of the oval from Oxford."

The reference to long hair took on significance when the teams went on the field. As did many players in football's early years, the Mississippians let their hair grow long and thick to protect their heads in collisions.

Decades later in a letter reminiscing about the game, substitute end Ralph Black would recall that the Mississippi players protested Sewanee's leather headgear. But game officials, aware that helmets of various kinds were becoming commonplace in football, did nothing about the protests.

So, here was Sewanee, surely weary and bruised from the long road trip, still unbeaten and unscored on, playing for the fifth straight time on an enemy field and taking on a team comparatively rested and eager to end Sewanee's victory string at eight games, four of them in the previous five days.

The *Commercial-Appeal* reporter described the moment just before the kickoff: "As the bandaged boys in purple took their positions, Coach Suter applied fresh plaster over the cut which Seibels received in the Texas game. The sight of the Sewanee men as they stood ready for the referee's whistle was enough to create a wholesome respect for them."

As in the first four games on the trip, Sewanee had many supporters in the crowd. The *Commercial-Appeal* reported in that morning's issue: "Today's game will be the last one of the trip, and great interest centers in the result, extending beyond the rank and file of collegians and football enthusiasts. For many years it has been a matter of much speculation as to whether the local alumni of the University of Mississippi exceeded that of any other college. The Sewanee followers think that they number the largest and have organized in a body to attend the game this afternoon."

The article named Sewanee alumni who would gather at the Peabody Hotel and accompany the team to the grounds in tally-hos. Memphis society people attended the game, led by Episcopal Bishop Thomas Frank Gailor, who of course cheered for the Purple. Reported the *Commercial-Appeal*: "Traps and turnouts were large in number and laden with the culture and beauty of Memphis' swell set."

Sometimes overlooked when the five-games trip is recounted is the fact that Ole Miss came within a few seconds of spoiling Sewanee's triumphant tour—not by defeating, but by tieing. Sewanee scored its first-half touchdown with only 15 seconds remaining and its second-half touchdown with but 13 seconds left in the game in a 12-0 win.

The pre-game story listed these starters:

Sewanee—Sims, left end; Jones, left tackle; Keyes, left guard; Poole, center; Claiborne, right guard; Bolling, right tackle; Pearce, right end; Wilson, quarterback; Seibels, left halfback; Kilpatrick, right halfback; Simkins, fullback.

Mississippi—Henry, left end; Farish, left tackle; Wright, left guard; Wainwright, center; White, right guard; Hall, right tackle; Foster, right end; Beanland, quarterback; Harvey, left halfback; Bass, right halfback; Myers, fullback.

The Sewanee halfback starters were reversed in that listing. Seibels was a fixture at right half and Kilpatrick had become the regular at left half.

Mallory and Rhea were listed as game officials. Game time was the customary 3:30.

The *Sewanee Purple* ran this game summary:

Sewanee defeated the University of Mississippi in Memphis on Nov. 14th, and by doing so has established a record in football annals which is likely to stand for years to come.

We all know how the Varsity took the long and tedious journey to Austin, and we likewise know the results of that game, and also the succeeding ones.

The team reached Memphis just after the Baton Rouge game, and after some sight-seeing they donned the moleskin for the fifth time with a determination to do or die.

That their efforts were successful the detailed account of the game will show. Mississippi never gained the required distance but once, and the game was principally played in her territory. During the first half, however, the Oxonians had succeeded in doing what but two teams have done this season, i.e., in crossing Sewanee's 30-yard line, Texas being the other successful eleven in accomplishing this feat.

The Memphis Commercial-Appeal, *under date of Nov. 15th, had the following to say of Sewanee:*

"Yesterday's score against the University of Mississippi marked the two hundred and fortieth point which the Tennesseans have scored to nothing for their opponents, during the present season. The trip of the Sewanee eleven, along with the record, will probably remain unequalled for many generations.

"The wisdom of arranging a trip from Middle Tennessee to

Texas and return, which included five games of football in six days, a change of diet, water, etc., was the subject of much discussion among people interested in football, but coach Suter and his little band have accomplished the task with few injuries or mishaps, and it is a foregone conclusion that the Cumberland mountains in the immediate vicinity of Sewanee will echo the welcome extended the wearers of the purple when they arrive home today."

The starting lineup printed in the *Purple* was the same for Sewanee, but was different in three or four positions for Mississippi, with Clapp at quarterback, Chandler instead of Bass at halfback, McIntyre instead of Wright at guard.

At some point in the action, Ralph Black substituted for Bunny Pearce at end for Sewanee. A half century later in a letter to Diddy Seibels he recalled: "We kicked till us ends were tired....Well do I remember Poole trying to pick me up in the backfield. Why don't you go for a touchdown (he asked), that was after I had dived on the ball on fumble by their back after I tackled him. (The) field (was) open but me, I did exactly as Coach Suter said, dive on the ball and don't lose it."

The *Purple's* play by play account:

Mississippi won the toss and chose the south goal, which was favored by a strong wind. Kilpatrick kicks off 40 yards. Mississippi then tried to penetrate the purple line, but found opposition and was forced to punt. Kilpatrick made a slight gain around right tackle, and then (past) Hall for 10 yards.

Seibels failed to gain, and then a fumble occurred. Mississippi was penalized for holding, however, and Sewanee was given the ball. Kilpatrick then went outside of right tackle for 10 yards, and Seibels advanced the ball to the 25-yard line. Wilson failed to gain on the next play, and later there was another fumble.

Chandler was then pushed over Jones for a small gain, and Mississippi made her one noteworthy gain, when Harvey went between Jones and Sims for 8 yards. White was stopped in his tracks, and on a fake kick Jones broke through and downed Hall with a loss of 10 yards. Myers then punted 30 yards, and Simkins fumbled. Hall made 2 yards through Jones, Myers bucked center for a small gain and with but a yard to gain, and the ball was on

Sewanee's 25-yard line.

The Varsity took a firm brace and secured the ball on downs. Here the distance was close and a measurement was called for. The referee's ruling proved correct, however, and Sewanee retained the ball. On the line-up Mississippi was given the ball, as a Sewanee man was holding.

The ball again went over to Sewanee on downs. Seibels then circled left end for 10 yards, and Kilpatrick passed Henry for 3 yards. Seibels goes outside of left tackle for 4 yards, and Kilpatrick plants 10 to the good. Mississippi again received the ball on Sewanee's holding, and after two futile attempts they were forced to punt.

Sewanee fumbled on the line-up, and Harvey fell on the ball. Myers then fumbled and Sims saved the ball for Sewanee. Seibels and Kilpatrick, by good gains, worked the ball down to the 10-yard line, where a fumble occurred and Foster fell on the ball a few feet from the goal line.

Myers punted out of danger to Simkins, who brought the ball back 10 yards. Seibels went through right tackle for 5 yards, and Wilson circled left end for 10. Seibels skirts left end for 10 yards and a touchdown. Sims kicks goal. Time: 24 minutes. Time was called here before the ball could be put into play.

Second half

Black replaced Pearce at right end, and later in the game Montgomery succeeded Henry. Myers kicks off 40 yards and Simkins comes back 15. Simkins then punts 35 yards, and after two trials Mississippi has to punt.

Kilpatrick goes around Henry for 10 yards, and Simkins punted to the middle of the field. Mississippi again found the impenetrable line awaiting her, Myers punted 30 yards, and Seibels fumbled, Henry falling on the ball. Mississippi again couldn't gain, and Myers punted to Sewanee's 5-yard line. Seibels passed Foster for 12 yards, and Kilpatrick goes through tackle for 4.

Small gains carried the ball to the center of the field, and Jones makes a pretty run of 35 yards, Seibels dashes around left end for 20 yards, and later made a good gain around Foster.

Sewanee fumbles on the next play, and a Mississippi man falls on the ball. Sewanee then gets the ball on a forward pass (Editor's note: Possibly meaning a fumble on a handoff), and Kilpatrick passes Henry for 10 yards. Sewanee was again penalized and the ball went over.

Myers punted poorly for 15 yards. Jones brings the ball to the 15-yard line on the next play, and Seibels goes his length through Hall. Kilpatrick is then given the ball, and he passes Hall for (the) second touchdown. Sims kick goal.

Time was called shortly after the teams lined up, and Sewanee had won her ninth game.

XII

Cliffhanger with Heisman: Sewanee 11, Auburn 10

Sewanee's place in football history now was assured. The five victories in six days, all on the road against name schools and without an opposition point, had assured the university everlasting recognition, although that recognition was decades in jelling.

Would more games, with the possibility of defeat or tie and opposition points, make the season less memorable, less worthy of a place in the record books? Games with Cumberland, Auburn and North Carolina would provide the answer.

Six days after the triumphant homecoming, Sewanee hosted Cumberland University at rocky Hardee Field. Had the Texas trip drained Sewanee to the point that underdog Cumberland might pull an upset? Remarkably the squad had come through the five games without crippling injuries and its starting lineup virtually intact. The summer-long conditioning had paid off.

Cumberland was a softie. Kilpatrick led a Sewanee touchdown parade with five, Seibels scored three, Wilson two, Jones and Bolling one each, and Sims kicked 11 of 12 points-after in a 71-0 runaway.

Sewanee now had 10 days, its longest rest of the season, to prepare for Auburn, coached by John Heisman, for whom football's prized trophy would be named. The 10 days may have given Sewanee the razor-thin edge at Montgomery, but a bitterly disappointed Heisman would dispute that.

Auburn had fielded its first team in 1892, defeating Georgia 10-0 in what would become one of America's top football rivalries. The Tigers, as they would be known, won two and lost two that first year, then went unbeaten in 1893 with wins over Alabama (twice) and Vanderbilt and ties with Sewanee and Georgia Tech.

Only 1894 was a losing season on the Plain. The following year John William Heisman took over the coaching and football down South was about to change. A native Pennsylvanian, Heisman had played as a lineman at first Brown, then Penn. He had planned to practice law but was drawn to football coaching.

After stints at Buchtel (now Akron) and Oberlin, both in Ohio, he chose to head south, as did so many other Eastern coaches. A tough-minded, eccentric perfectionist, Heisman would lay down the law to his players with such observations as

—Better to have died a small boy than to fumble the football.

—When you find a weak spot in the defense, hammer it.

—When in doubt about what play to call, punt.

—Don't cuss, don't argue with officials, and don't lose.

In time, Heisman would be credited with being first to use the hidden ball trick and with getting the forward pass approved. He is still mentioned along with such giants as Walter Camp, Alonzo Stagg and Pop Warner for his contributions to early football.

After his Auburn years, he would move on to coaching success at Clemson and Georgia Tech.

In his book *Heroes of the Heisman Trophy*, Bill Libby wrote that Heisman either originated or was among the first to use

—vocal signals ("hike" or "hep") to put the ball into play

—the long center snapback instead of rolling the ball back

—backfield shifts

—laterals.

Heisman was described as a gentleman, a coach with chemistry to instill spirit in his players.

In 1899 Heisman was a young coach heading from Auburn to Montgomery to try knocking off high-riding Sewanee. His Auburn team came within a whisker of doing just that, and Heisman insisted afterward that poor officiating, not Sewanee skill, had done in his team.

In its pre-game story the *Montgomery Advertiser* described the matchup as the greatest in Southern athletics. Advance ticket sales at several stores had been brisk and the *Advertiser's* Squire Brown wrote "it will be a difficult matter today to secure a trap, drag or vehicle of any description while the street cars will have all they can do."

As Memphis already was for Ole Miss, Montgomery was a second home for the Auburn team; that meant the crowd would be predominantly pro-Auburn. But Sewanee would have strong support, partly because team captain Diddy Seibels had grown up in Montgomery and the Seibelses and Goldthwaites (his mother's family) were still prominent there.

Sewanee carried a small weight advantage, but Auburn was a strong, seasoned team that already had proved it could hold its own with heavier teams. Its "crack" quarterback Huguley (the *Advertiser's* adjective) was playing his fourth year.

Auburn may have had a coaching edge with Heisman in his fourth year at the Loveliest Village, but Suter's men—with their customary early-summer practice start—had had several more weeks to condition and to polish plays and already had played 10 games to Auburn's four.

Kickoff time was 2:30, the place was Montgomery's Oak Park on a field used during the summer for professional baseball. By the time the teams lined up, 4,000 fans either had taken their seats or were standing close along the sidelines.

Game officials were William Pirrie Taylor of Birmingham, a Yale man and school principal, umpire, and a Mr. Martin of the University of Virginia, referee.

In his history of Southern football, sportswriter Fuzzy Woodruff, who saw the game, recalled, "Under Heisman"s tutelage, Auburn played with a marvelous speed and dash that couldn't be gainsaid and which fairly swept Sewanee off its feet. Only the remarkable punting of Simkins kept the game from being a debacle.

"I recall vividly one incident of the game, which demonstrates clearly just how surprising was Sewanee's victory.

"The Purple was taking time out. They began this early in the game, when their athletes appeared tired and worn whereas Auburn men were full of fight and fire.

"A Sewanee player was down, his head being bathed....Suter, the Sewanee coach, and Heisman, the Auburn mentor, were walking up and down the field together.

"They approached this boy. The rules were not as rigid then I guess against coaches encroaching on the field of play or conversing with players, or anyhow they were not enforced for Suter, evidently as mad as fire, asked the down and out player 'Are you fellows going to be run over like this all afternoon?'

" 'Coach,' said the boy, lifting his tired head from the ground, 'we just can't stand this stuff. We've never seen anything like it.'

"Suter and Heisman turned away. 'Can you beat that?' Suter asked the Auburn coach. Heisman didn't say anything. I guess he thought a great deal.

"He told me afterwards that he had never felt so sorry for a man on a football field as he had for Suter at that moment."

In its February 1900 wrapup of the '99 season, *Outing* magazine would report: "For the only time during the season Sewanee found herself on the defensive from the opening of the game....Auburn played with dash and spirit, and, in ground gaining, they excelled the Tennessee team, while on defense they were evenly matched."

The hotly contested game ultimately turned on a disputed decision by Umpire Taylor by which he awarded ball possession to Sewanee. Soon thereafter, Sewanee scored the tieing touchdown, kicked the point-after and won the day 11-10.

Heisman cried foul, both at the game and in a letters-to-the-editor debate with Umpire Taylor (details in next chapter). For a long time the outcome was a sore spot with Heisman and Auburn. Heisman insisted that no matter how many times the teams played, Auburn would win every time.

What was Sewanee's response? Lucky to get out of Montgomery a winner for sure, but with ready rebuttal to Heisman. The injured player who had told Suter, "We just can't stand this stuff. We've never seen anything like it," may have been referring—rather than to a physical pounding by Auburn—to what he and his teammates considered illegal tactics. The *Sewanee Purple's* game account said as much, with specifics.

Sewanee alumnus James Young, who many years later got to know both Suter and Heisman in New York, recalled that Suter told him Heisman "had pulled some much-too-tricky stuff on Sewanee in that battle—his players on several occasions grabbed the ball when it was dead and dashed down the field for a touchdown (called back, of course); and he had his players lock arms, on end sweeps, so that it was almost impossible to break through and bring down the runner. He said that to stop that monkey-business, he had his ends...go in feet first and smack those interferers!" So Sewanee also appeared to have gotten in some questionable licks.

In another letter to reserve end Ralph Black a half century later, Young referred to Heisman as a "very fine man...a thoroughly honorable sportsman....When I knew him, he was wonderful, a grand human being."

Another factor that should help put Auburn's spirited play in perspective: Perhaps Sewanee's game experience on the Texas trip—hard but clean play and sportsmanship throughout—may have lulled the players into expecting the same from Auburn. From Fuzzy Woodruff's description of the game, Auburn was fired up from the opening whistle and never let up, gaining the momentum and keeping Sewanee on the defensive. Whether the often-fine line between fair and foul was crossed was up to the officials. Indications were that they more than earned their pay that day.

Did Heisman's men get the short end on officiating? He was adamant they did. Did Auburn violate fair-play rules? Sewanee was just as adamant.

The starting lineups in Woodruff's account:

Auburn—Thomas, left end; Braswell, left tackle; Butler, left guard, Guin, center; Martin, right guard; Harvey, right tackle; Park, right end; Huguley, quarterback; Skeggs, right halfback; Feagin, left halfback, Bivens, fullback.

Sewanee—Pearce, left end; Jones, left tackle; Claiborne, left guard; Poole, center; Keyes, right guard; Bolling, right tackle; Sims, right end; Wilson, quarterback; Seibels, right halfback; Kilpatrick, left halfback; Simkins, full-back.

Black and Hull were listed as Sewanee substitutes.

The *Advertiser* account of the game was written by Squire Brown, a pen name for W.W. Screws, Jr., which concluded with a paragraph about a Sewanee alumni banquet that night for the players. Toasts were offered in clear water, "the team not yet being out of training."

The Squire Brown game story, except for several paragraphs of a lengthy pre-game description, follows.

For the first time this season the Sewanee goal line was crossed yesterday and in a manner that brought on several very pro-nounced cases of the most acute heart failure.

Within about twelve minutes after the umpire's whistle started off the first half, an athletic looking chap darts out from the tangled mass of padded humanity and by a great run of twelve yards managed to get over the line, falling exhausted on the first touchdown that has been made against the Purple this year.

As if by magic, a long, loud roar arose from the Orange and Blue enthusiasts and for a space pandemonium reigned, pandemonium of the wildest enthusiasm—the hitherto impregnable Purple line had been crossed and at least once a score had been registered against it.

It was recorded that that score of the Orange and Blue was to be duplicated and the only thing in all the world that gave the Purple the big end of the final score was that strong, sure kick of Sims, Sewanee's left end, when he put that leather spheroid over the posts for a goal in the second period.

Never before has such a scene taken place in the South as was presented on the streets of Montgomery and out at the ball park yesterday. Very early in the day it was when Auburn boys began moving about and groups of them showed up all round, the inevitable college yell from their lusty young lungs bringing a smile of sympathy and a memory of old college days to men who had traveled all along the self-same route.

The union station (Editor: depot) was the mecca about 10 o'clock and a little after that time there was a perfect jam of Auburn boys.

The Purple was much in evidence though, for numbers of ladies were there to meet Manager Lea and his team from the faraway Tennessee mountains.

Soon the excursion train on the Western came in loaded to the guards with several hundred college boys and ladies and gentlemen from different stations between here and Atlanta.

The feature of the train was an immense billy goat completely wrapped about with Auburn's colors....

Not very long had the impatient crowd to wait before the regular Western train arrived and in their sleeper attached to the end of the train was the Sewanee team. Cheer after cheer arose as they came through the gates, the Auburn boys yelling as heartily as the Sewanee enthusiasts and a triumphal march was commenced up Commerce Street.

Never before has the historic old Exchange Hotel witnessed the equal of the scenes that took place in the lobby. From then until lunch time a mass of college boys shouting, yelling and doing everything that only college boys can do, completely filling every nook and cranny of the lobby.

A little after 12 o'clock it was that the crowds began pouring out to the grounds, and such crowds. (Editor's note: Brown's pre-game description ran on and on, noting that the Sewanee squad had arrived after a hard overnight ride, had gotten a few hours of rest, then gone to the playing field.)

The game in detail

Sewanee won the toss and chose the South goal with the wind at her back.

At 2:55 o'clock, sharp, the referee's whistle blew, and the game was on. Braswell, Auburn's big tackle, kicks the ball to Sewanee's ten yard line, the ball is brought back five yards by Seibels.

(Editor's note: Brown's story had an obvious omission at this point.)

The ball is given to Feagin who makes three yards through the Sewanee line. Bivens, the big Auburn fullback, goes five yards through tackle, the ball is fumbled, however, and a Sewanee man falls on it.

Simkins gets five yards through the Auburn line, they try bucking the line again with no gain, they then try Auburn's right end but are thrown back with no gain and the ball goes over. (Editor: Another omission here.)

Simkins gets two yards through the Auburn line. Simkins gets four through tackle and again three around end. He tries again without any gain and is hurt.

Kilpatrick tries the Auburn line but makes no impression, and again the Sewanee backs fail to gain and the ball goes over on downs.

Skeggs gets a fine run around right end for ten yards. Bivens tears off five through tackle. Feagin gets five yards through tackle and Bivens four over center, while Park gets four around the end.

Skeggs gets fifteen yards on a fine run around left end, superb interference being given him by Huguley, the plucky Auburn quarterback, who is playing a star game. Feagin then makes a fine fifteen-yard run with splendid interference and the ball is on Sewanee's ten-yard line. Two more line bucks by Auburn and the ball is on Sewanee's four-yard line. Auburn is playing a lightning game and the game is all her way so far.

Auburn then tried a quarterback kick, Sewanee man caught (it) and it is Sewanee's ball on her three-yard line. (Editor's note: Apparently Auburn tried a field goal, which was unsuccessful).

Kilpatrick gets one yard through tackle, the ball is fumbled, but a Sewanee man falls on it. Simkins then kicks forty yards. Auburn's ball.

Park gets three yards through the Sewanee line, Braswell one yard while Feagin gets eight yards around end, and Park four yards around the other end. Huguley then gets a fine run around Sewanee's right end for fifteen yards; Auburn tries (a) trick play, no gain; Bivens tears off eight yards through right guard, and Feagin on a double pass (Editor: Double handoff) gets in a twelve-yard run to a touchdown. It was a beautiful run and the wildest of enthusiasm followed, it being the first time this season that the Sewanee goal line had been crossed. The Auburn rooters' hopes were dashed, however, when the referee called the ball back and stated that it was an offside play.

Skeggs then goes over tackle for three yards on a line buck. Auburn again tries the Sewanee line but fails to gain. Bivens then tears his way through the Sewanee line for a touchdown. The pandemonium that followed was something, the Auburn rooters fairly going wild with joy. Huguley then kicks out and the ball is caught, but is claimed not heeled by the Auburn man, and it is no goal.

(Editor's note: Because not making the extra point was so costly to Auburn, this researcher tried to determine what rule infraction was involved. In those days, if a player sought to make a "fair catch" while receiving a "kick out," he had to mark with his heel the spot where he was catching the ball.)

(After a team had scored a touchdown and before it attempted the extra-point kick, it had to "kick out" and fair catch the ball. Included in the fair catch was the requirement to heel the ball. An official ruled Auburn did not do that and was not entitled to the usual try for point from the 25-yard line).

Score Auburn 5, Sewanee 0 after eighteen minutes playing time.

Sewanee then kicks to Auburn's ten yard line, the ball is brought back seven yards; the lines then crash together, and instantly the agile figure of Huguley, Auburn's quarterback, shoots out and is down the field for forty yards before he is tackled by Seibels. The ball, however, is brought back, the referee claiming the play was made after he had blown his whistle. It is Sewanee's ball. The Auburn men are kicking vigorously over the referee's decision and do not understand why the ball should go over to Sewanee. He holds to his decision, however, and it is Sewanee's ball on Auburn's seventeen yard line.

Simkins gets two yards through the Auburn line. Seibels gets three and Kilpatrick two. The ball is now on Auburn's ten-yard line. Sewanee tries the line without a gain and Kilpatrick makes one yard through tackle. Sewanee is then thrown back one yard on a line buck. (Editor: A penalty must have occurred at this point; otherwise, the ball would have gone over to Auburn on downs.) Seibels then goes over tackle for two yards. The ball is then given to Kilpatrick, who jumps through and over the Auburn line for a touchdown. The Sewanee contingent being jubilant. Sims misses goal and the score is 5 to 5.

Hull takes place of Simkins, who is hurt.

Braswell then kicks off to Sewanee's 15-yard line. Auburn's ends are down the field like lightning, however, and the Sewanee back gets only three yards. Sewanee kicks thirty yards and it is Auburn's ball.

Skeggs goes at tackle but makes no gain. Huguley then gets in another of his sensational runs for twenty yards. Bivens goes through the Sewanee line for seven yards, while Feagin gets four in the same place. Feagin then makes a ten-yard gain at right end while Bivens goes over tackle for five yards. Bivens then goes against the Sewanee line on a tackle buck for a touchdown. Huguley then kicks out, the ball is heeled, and Auburn has a try for goal. The kick is nicely blocked by Claiborne, the big Sewanee guard, and the score stands: Auburn 10, Sewanee 5.

Sims kicks off for Sewanee, the ball rolling across Auburn's goal line; it is brought back to Auburn's fifteen-yard line and put in play.

Skeggs gets five yards around end and Feagin gets four in the same place. Bivens then bucks the line for two yards, and Feagin makes a ten yard run around end, aided by splendid interference; Huguley then makes three yards on a trick play, and Bivens gets one yard through guard.

Auburn then makes two ineffectual bucks at the Sewanee line, and the ball goes over on downs. Sewanee here punted forty yards and Wilson, her fleet footed little quarterback, fell on it on Auburn's five yard line.

Kilpatrick then gets four yards through the Auburn line, and Simkins tries with no gain. Seibels here tries an end run which is quickly stopped by a tackle by Thomas with a loss of one yard, and the ball is Auburn's on downs.

Bivens is sent against the Sewanee line for four yards. Auburn then fumbles and Martin, Auburn's right guard, falls on it.

Here a mighty kick was registered by the Auburn team. The umpire, however, stuck to his decision and the ball was Sewanee's on Auburn's fifteen yard line. (Editor's note: The "mighty kick" in this case obviously meant a strong protest.) Here Sewanee scores a touchdown on a trick play, sending Wilson around left end for a touchdown. Sims kicked goal and the score stands Sewanee 11, Auburn 10.

Auburn now kicks to Sewanee's five-yard line, and the ball is brought back seven yards by Kilpatrick. Seibels gets four yards around end, and Jones five. Kilpatrick then makes five more and Seibels fails to gain.

Simkins then gets three yards on a fake buck, and the referee's whistle blows with the ball on Sewanee's twenty-five yard line, and the first half is over, and the score, Sewanee 11, Auburn 10.

Second half

Sims kicks off to Auburn's 15-yard line, the Sewanee ends are down the field in a hurry, and Auburn gets only three yards.

Feagin makes five yards around end, and follows it with three more through the line. Bivens then makes two through tackle. Skeggs here makes a long run of twenty yards around Sewanee's right end.

Bivens tried the line with no gain and Feagin gets five yards around end.

Park now gets seven around end. Auburn fumbles and the ball is Sewanee's. Seibels tries end run, is tackled however by Harvey who breaks through the line and (Seibels is) thrown for a loss of three yards.

Seibels is given the ball and makes a good run around end; he is tackled nicely by Sloan. Sewanee kicks and Huguley brings it back fifteen yards behind splendid interference.

Auburn tried the Sewanee line again but gets nothing, and again an end run is thrown back by Sims with a loss of one yard. The ball now goes over to Sewanee on downs.

Kilpatrick gets one yard through tackle. Seibels then tried same place but is thrown back with no gain. Sewanee here kicks, and her end is down the field quickly and it is Sewanee's ball. Here Kilpatrick tries an end run; he is nicely tackled by Harvey, who brings him to earth with a small gain.

Seibels tries end and gets nothing; he then bucks the line for three yards. Kilpatrick tries the Auburn line but without success. Seibels then tried Auburn's line but is tackled beautifully by Park with a loss of one yard.

Hull kicks out and it is Auburn's ball near center of the field. Bivens bucks the Sewanee line for thirteen yards. Auburn fails to gain on next three downs, and gets three through center on next play. The ball there goes over on downs.

Sewanee fumbles and it is Auburn's ball. Here Sloan, Auburn's halfback, circled the Sewanee end for fifteen yards.

It was now almost dark, and Referee Martin called the game with the ball in Auburn's possession in center of the field.

Only about fourteen minutes of the second half were played, owing to so much time being taken by lay-puts (Editor's note: Presumably, pileups and slowness in unpiling and wrangles over the two officials' decisions.)

Sewanee played a splendid game and showed that her team was all that has been said of her, while Auburn showed clearly that their team is able to cope with that of any in the South, and it was only through her quick, snappy, and heady playing that she succeeded in doing what no team has done this season, score against the Sewanee team.

It is hard to say who played the star games for either side, but for Sewanee, Seibels, Wilson, Sims and Kilpatrick played brilliantly, while for Auburn Huguley, Park, Feagin, Bivens, Skeggs and Harvey played especially well.

XIII

Heisman versus the umpire

[H]ere (as chronicler Squire Brown would begin), a sidetrip from the Iron Men story. The purpose is twofold: (1) to illustrate the intense feelings that football aroused even in the game's pioneer years and (2) to provide a morsel of insight into John Heisman, the Auburn coach and pillar of the game.

People who agreed to officiate football in the 1880s and '90s were due much credit, even admiration. At best, the rules were murky and changing year to year. In the face of intimidating coaches and players, plus rabid fans who often spilled onto playing fields, impartial officiating required courage.

Trying almost a century later to weigh the merits of officials' interpretations of rules and coaches' protests during and after the Sewanee-Auburn game would avail nothing. And in their post-game newspaper debate, Heisman and Umpire William Pirrie Taylor were so intent on personal digs that they—intentionally or not—provided little to help readers understand the points at issue. The all-too-familiar case of much heat, little light.

Even so, their arguing in print surely made good reading and stirred endless post mortems among both people who attended the game and those who only read about it. Imagine how today's radio talk shows would have relished and fueled the fussing!

Heisman certainly needed no starter fluid, but the *Montgomery Advertiser's* Squire Brown provided it with this observation in a follow-up commentary: "There have been hundreds and hundreds of baseball, football and other games played, and I have yet to see the first one in which somebody on the defeated side did not ring in the old cry of fraud, and generally the loudest shouters of the swindling lay are people who know just about as much about the game they are watching as a pig does of the Ten Commandments. They hear somebody intimate such a thing, and, of course, like parrots they have to repeat it.

"I asked Mr. Heisman Thursday night after the game his opinion of it and he stated that they would enter a protest against the decision on that first (Auburn) run and touchdown; no other point did he mention though I asked him several times. Later I asked Mr. Taylor (the umpire) about that decision and he said that the run was made before the ball was put in play.

"Now about calling the game before the last half was finished," Brown's column continued. (Editor's note: The game was stopped because of darkness.) "Before the coin toss several ground rules were made and among them one providing that if it became too dark for further play the referee should give the two teams five minutes notice and at the end of five minutes, call the game no matter where the ball was or what state the game was in. Mr. Taylor gave the five minutes notice and at the end of five minutes called the game with the score standing 11-10 in favor of Sewanee." (Editor's note: Actually, Referee Martin—not Umpire Taylor—would have had the authority to declare the game over).

At this point background is in order and is provided by Fuzzy Woodruff's *History of Southern Football.* In Auburn's game earlier in the season with Georgia, darkness was coming on with Auburn leading 11-5 and moving the ball deep in Georgia territory. Less than two minutes remained on the clock, so Auburn had the game locked up. The referee stopped the game and announced the score would revert to 0-0 because darkness prevented completion. And that's the way it went into the record books. The umpire that day was William Pirrie Taylor, who would umpire Auburn-Sewanee.

A researcher of football officiating perhaps could reconcile the contradictory end-of-games calls, both of which left Heisman's Auburn with the short end of the stick. But it seems clear that if Heisman carried a chip on his shoulder into the Sewanee game and a matching chip on the other shoulder at game's end, he seems to have had cause.

In the umpire's behalf: Taylor later insisted that he had told Heisman a "no game" ruling would have been more appropriate as the Sewanee-Auburn score, but "this wouldn't suit the gentleman; it wouldn't win any bets." Actually the referee, a Virginian named Martin, had the authority to call the game because of darkness, but Heisman insisted that the referee was strongly swayed by Umpire Taylor on almost every critical call.

In a letter to the *Birmingham Age-Herald* on Monday after the Thanksgiving Day game, Heisman criticized Taylor for making calls that Heisman said were not his to make, but were the referee's, including one that enabled Sewanee to block a crucial point-after-touchdown attempt by Auburn.

Heisman also wrote that Taylor showed incompetence in measuring for first downs and that he knew little about football rules in general, especially when he took possession of the ball from Auburn and awarded it to Sewanee.

Heisman insisted that he bore no ill feelings toward Coach Billy Suter and the Sewanee players, but he asserted that Auburn could beat Sewanee if they played every day of the week.

Enter again Squire Brown, replying to Heisman's letter, and insisting he had done his best to report the game impartially, that he had too quoted Heisman correctly and that his story made plain Auburn had outplayed Sewanee—except for the score.

Umpire Taylor also read Heisman's letter and took pen in hand to respond.

The Birmingham school administrator wrote: "This professional coach, would-be 'actor of character parts' (to quote his own words to me), expert gambler in football futures, and would-be professor of elocution and oratory, considers the sporting world out of joint and that he, like Hamlet, is 'born to set it right.'

"His statement that he will not protest the game shows the lamentable weakness of his position.

"The plain truth of the matter is that Coach Heisman has proved a failure in producing winning teams at Auburn....Is it not most likely that he must keep in Auburn's good graces by ascribing defeats to the officials....?

"Does Mr. Heisman really forget that I called time so that I might cut off the straps from the belts of his players, straps which were used by his players to hold opponents illegally?....

"He quotes me as stating that I would not penalize Auburn because of my 'fear of the crowd.' ....I purposely overlooked Auburn's foul play, knowing the tension under which they were laboring, preferring to incur Sewanee's displeasure rather than let the game end in 'bad blood.'"

Taylor wrote that that was all he would say, that he would not respond to any Heisman rebuttal.

The coach rebutted immediately. "Mr. Taylor started in to throw mud at me instead of answering the points of football I discussed....

"Mr. Taylor intimates that I had money at stake on our games with Georgia and Sewanee. I emphatically state that I neither bet, won or lost a single cent on either of them....But Mr. Taylor's brother told a man now in Birmingham that he won money on the Auburn-Sewanee game, and yet that brother was presented to me by Mr. Taylor before the game as a prospective linesman for the game. I promptly and unhesitatingly accepted him, but Sewanee wanted and put in another man.

"Does Mr. Taylor forget that he stated last year in Atlanta...that I was the best coach in the South?....

"Mr. Taylor pleads for himself and against me; I plead for justice and the Auburn football team. Yours for competent officiating. J.W. Heisman."

The following season Heisman moved on to coach at Clemson, then to coaching success at Georgia Tech and ultimately to lasting attention as the man for whom the Heisman Trophy is named.

This researcher's efforts to trace Taylor's officiating career were not productive.

XIV

Goal-line iron:
Sewanee 5, Carolina 0

With scarcely time to catch their breath after the knockdown-dragout, come-from-behind-and-hang-on squeaker over Auburn, Sewanee's Iron Men lined up two days later to battle the University of North Carolina, called by some the South's top team.

The point already has been made that Sewanee's Dec. 2 matchup with Carolina in Atlanta was not an 11th-hour showdown arranged after the Purple's dramatic win at Montgomery on Thanksgiving Day. Some latter-day accounts of the '99 Sewanee season suggest that, but Carolina had been on Sewanee's schedule all season long. What *did* develop after the Auburn game was agreement by both sides that Sewanee vs. North Carolina would decide the Southern champion.

In later years someone decided it would be appropriate to call the winner-take-all meeting "the first bowl game." Perhaps *that* claim has merit.

Although no Sewanee injury list was disclosed after the bruising game with Auburn, the starting lineup against Carolina showed that Billy Suter had to juggle his starters because several were hurt seriously and the first-string ends did not start in Atlanta. The Auburn game alone apparently had taken a greater physical toll than the combined five games in six days.

Ormond Simkins and Diddy Seibels, two season-long mainstays, were among the injured at Montgomery, but both started against Carolina. Simkins must have really been hurting because he moved from his customary fullback spot to left end, replacing Bartlet Sims, and relinquishing the punting to Seibels. Ralph Black replaced Bunny Pearce at right end and Dan Hull started at fullback.

Thus the Sewanee lineup was revamped extensively for the first time since Suter had called the squad together back in September. Simkins' long spirals had kept opponents backed up all season, so Suter probably felt some concern there despite having seen Seibels handle the kicking occasionally.

The *Sewanee Purple's* game story reported that ideal weather with just a tinge of winter prevailed for the game at Atlanta's Piedmont Park. By 2:30, the *Purple* reported, "the bleachers were taxed to their utmost seating capacity, and the grandstand was comfortably filled with the fair sex; while on the south and east sides of the gridiron were the smart traps (carriages) containing the admirers of both teams."

The campus paper described the game as "replete with brilliant plays, startling sensations, and free from the many objectionable features which characterized the Auburn game."

Ralph Black, who had warmed the bench most of the Texas trip and was making his first start of the season, would reminisce about the game in a 1949 letter to Diddy Seibels. Whether Black was only relaying gossip or had witnessed what he described, he wrote Seibels that Auburn Coach John Heisman, who had gone to Atlanta to see the game, was "sore on being beat, etc., flashed a $100 bet that we would not beat N.C., then you will know how we (emptied) our pockets of dimes and dollars to cover every cent he had. How we had fun over this for we knew we would win."

Black also recalled a dance given for Sewanee that evening by his aunt, Mrs. Joseph Johnson, "at the fashionable Old Ball Room at the Kimball House" and "how we held N.C. for 9 downs inside our ten yd. line and then that marvelous kick by Kil (Rex Kilpatrick) from the 36 yd. line for the only score."

Black noted in the letter that Sewanee saw no more of Heisman after that "but (we) enjoyed spending his money on riotous living in Atlanta."

The Carolina coach, J.G. "Lady" Jayne, certainly was no stranger to the Sewanee players. He had resigned as

Sewanee coach only the year before and now would do battle with his onetime Princeton roommate and still-good friend, Billy Suter.

Just as Sewanee had, Carolina had played a demanding game only two days previously, defeating Georgia 5-0. The Tar Heel team had lost to two strong Eastern teams but was unbeaten against Southern teams, which explains the billing of the contest in Atlanta as for the Southern championship.

An Atlanta newspaper reported: "The feature which gave the game its beauty and raised it above the ordinary mass play contest was the wonderful punting of Seibels for Sewanee....The work of Seibels all the way through was above the ordinary, as the bulk of the gains for his team was made by him."

Umpire for the game was William Pirrie Taylor of Birmingham. If Auburn's John Heisman *did* risk a sizable sum on Carolina to win, as Ralph Black reported, Heisman probably kept a close eye on the umpire's calls.

The starting lineups:

Carolina—Craig, left end; Capt. Shull, left tackle; Brem, left guard; Elliott, center; Phifer, right guard; Bennett, right tackle; Osborne, right end; Martin, quarterback; Koehler, left halfback; Bellamy, right halfback; Graves, fullback.

Sewanee—Simkins, left end; Jones, left tackle; Keyes, left guard; Poole, center; Claiborne, right guard; Bolling, right tackle; Black, right end; Wilson, quarterback; Kilpatrick, left halfback; Capt. Seibels, right halfback; Hull, fullback.

Substitutes: Carolina—McKeever, Osborne. Sewanee—Gray.

The *Sewanee Purple* carrid this play-by-play account:

It was nearly three o'clock when Graves sent the pigskin to Sewanee's 10-yard line, and on the lineup, Seibels punted 40 yards. Koehler then gets four yards outside of right tackle, and adds two more on a quick opening. Graves goes through right for one yard, and Koehler left tackle for two.

Carolina then fumbles, and it is Sewanee's ball. Seibels gets three yards on a mass on tackle, and Hull punts twenty-five. Bellamy gets one yard around left end, and Graves punts twenty-

five. Seibels fumbles and a Carolina man falls on it.

Phifer makes two and Bellamy three yards, and Carolina is given ten yards on an offside play. Bellamy gains three yards, but drops the ball and a Sewanee man falls on it, and Seibels then punts fifty yards.

On the lineup, Graves punts the ball, only going thirty yards. Wilson fumbles, however, and Brem falls on the ball. Bellamy gets four yards, Koehler four and Bellamy one. Koehler adds two and Carolina is given ten more on an offside. Bellamy fails to gain. Koehler goes over tackle for five, he follows with four at the same point, and the ball is on the five-yard line.

Sewanee is offside and half the distance is given to Carolina. Koehler bucks for one yard, and Sewanee is again offside, and Carolina is given half the distance to goal line, and the ball is on the twelve-inch line.

Here occurred the magnificent defense spoken of elsewhere, and Carolina knows she had lost the ball (Editor: Probably "ballgame."). Sewanee gets the ball on downs and Seibels punts forty-five yards.

Carolina gets twelve yards on four plays, and as they are near the twenty-five yard line, Brem falls back and tries a drop kick (Editor's note: Explained earlier as a one-man effort equivalent to a place kick). The ball sails to the left of the goal posts, and is brought to the twenty-five yard line, and Seibels kicks forty yards.

Graves then punts thirty-five yards, and Seibels returns ten. Sewanee gets ten yards on Carolina's holding. Hull gets four yards through center and Kilpatrick six yards in two attempts. Seibels then punts thirty-five yards, and on the line-up Graves punts thirty.

Hull makes a quick kick for forty yards, the ball rolling behind the goal posts. Carolina brings it out and Graves punts thirty-five yards and Seibels fumbles, Carolina securing the ball and Graves punts thirty yards to Simkins. Sewanee makes ten yards on three plays and Seibels punts forty yards.

Graves punts back thirty yards, and Seibels punts same distance. Sewanee then gets the ball for holding, and sends Jones around right end for twenty yards. Kilpatrick gains three but drops the ball, and Carolina gets it ten yards from her goal.

Graves then punts twenty-five yards. Simkins signals for a fair catch, but Osborne tackles him, and Sewanee gets fifteen yards and a place kick. The ball is twenty-two yards from the goal and amid breathless suspense Kilpatrick sends it between the posts and Sewanee has clinched the game. (Editor's note: The "clinched" reference appears premature, but this account was written long after the game.)

Score: Sewanee 5, Carolina 0.

Second half

The second half was a punting game throughout, Sewanee being principally on the defensive.

Carolina worked hard for a touchdown, and had the ball on the ten-yard line when time was called. Her men realized that a touchdown and goal would mean a victory, and they worked desperately for this end. Sewanee, however, realized her position, and with five points to the good, they kept the ball in the air most of the time.

The features of this half were the long runs of Howells (Editor: Obviously a substitute the Purple reporter failed to list), which netted forty-five yards, and a kick Jones blocked, which rolled behind Carolina's goal line.

Sewanee gets in scoring distance twice; once on the ten-yard line and once on the fourteen-yard line. In each instance, however, the Carolinians put up a brilliant defense, and secured the ball on downs.

Sewanee punted fifteen times in the second half, with a total of three hundred and eighty yards, and an average punt of nearly thirty-nine yards (Editor's note: Either Sewanee punted fewer times or her statistician added incorrectly; no matter, Seibels apparently had averaged around 40 yards per kick during the season, and probably kicked that well against Carolina. The Atlanta Constitution reporter seemed to think so.).

Carolina punted ten times, with a total of three hundred and thirty yards and an average punt of thirty-three yards.

For another view of the game, following is the full account carried in the *Atlanta Constitution*:

On an ideal football day and in the closest contest ever seen on an Atlanta gridiron, Sewanee yesterday wrested victory from the stubborn eleven of North Carolina and placed the proud purple of the Tennessee college at the summit of the championship pole.

The score of five to nothing in which the final game of the season ended does not tell accurately of the evenly matched strength of the two elevens, although no one will begrudge Sewanee the five points that made her the champion and to which she was entitled by the brilliance of her defense.

The purple is today the proudest color in half a hundred southern colleges, the strongest teams of which the Tennessee boys have met and defeated, while the rest register below the purple by reason of their defeat at the hands of minor colleges. Georgia, Auburn and North Carolina, the recognized leaders in the southern athletic field, have one by one gone the way of all the southern football world before the fast, well trained sportsmanlike team of Sewanee that has from the first to last had only victory and no defeat. Notwithstanding the uninterrupted victories of Sewanee over the three colleges named, it would be hard to find anywhere in the country four elevens more evenly matched and made up than the four which the public of Atlanta have had the opportunity of seeing.

The team from Sewanee came on the field yesterday in splendid physical condition and to this as much as anything else the Tennessee boys can attribute the victory over a somewhat crippled adversary.

In the first half of the contest as the result of an exchange of punts and bad muffs on the part of Sewanee backs, the oval found itself within one yard of the purple goal line, and the great crowd in the grandstand and bleachers stood up to see the spheroid carried over for a touchdown.

There were probably none who doubted that Carolina would make the best of such an advantage and the wearers of the purple contented themselves by saying the game was yet young. But there was no touchdown, for the sturdy Tennesseans gritted their teeth and stood in their last ditch with the strength of men whose lives depended on the next rush.

Five times the Carolina backs were hurled with tremendous force against the line and each time they were thrown back without gaining an inch. While in this trying and desperate position Sewanee was twice penalized for off side playing, and at each offense of this character the ball was declared on its first down.

The Carolina backs were all given the oval in succession and for tries at different parts of the line, but the same result followed each attempt. Halfback Koehler, who on Thursday distinguished himself by the brilliance of his runs, was pushed into the line with towering force, seemed to cross it but was shoved back by the *tiger-like defense of the Sewanee men.*

Nothing like that defense has ever been seen on an Atlanta gridiron. It gave the Sewanee team the confidence it was sorely in need of, and informed Carolina more surely than could words that the crossing of the purple goal was anything but a mild undertaking.

The Carolinians immediately recognized the difficulty of the task, as was shown a few moments later when on Sewanee's thirty yard line, Drew tried a goal from the field, the ball going to the left of the post some eight or ten feet.

During the remainder of the first half the ball was kept almost continually in North Carolina territory solely as a result of the magnificent kicking of Seibels. Not once during the game did Sewanee get within ten yards of Carolina's goal and the five points scored to her credit came more as a penalty for the Tarheels' foul tackling than to the ground gaining qualities of the Sewanee backs.

The two teams were lined up on Carolina's fifteen yard line and Graves was given the ball to kick it out of danger. Simkins, who was playing back for Tennessee, signaled for a fair chance and as the ball fell into his arms he kneeled. Osborne, of North Carolina, came down on him regardless of the signal and the umpire immediately gave Sewanee fifteen yards and a free kick from the field.

The oval sailed safely through the goal posts and Sewanee had her five points.

The strength displayed by Carolina in the second half after the exhausted appearance of her men in the first, was the surprise of the game.

Captain Shull, one of the strongest supports of the line, was compelled to retire in the early part of the second half with a badly wrenched knee, but his place was well filled, and Sewanee seemed to gain nothing by the exchange.

With only five minutes to play Carolina came to her best strength and had she played throughout with the same display of vim and determination exhibited in the last few rushes, there might have been a victory to her credit by a safe score.

New life was put into Carolina when Howell was given a place back of the line as time and again the wiry young Trojan dashed for splendid gains through the purple forwards and finally when time was called had carried the oval all the way in triumph from Carolina's twenty yard line to dangerously near Sewanee's goal.

The prettiest run of the contest was that of Howell when he was given the oval for a dash around the end, the ball at the time well within Carolina's territory. With a bound he was away from the mass of players in an instant, leaving his own interference with the exception of one runner and making a bee line for Sewanee's goal. More than one Sewanee man went down before the stiff arm shoves delivered by the lithe, struggling Howell as he turned and twisted through a maze of players like a well-oiled Indian. (Editor: Engine?)

Score, 5 to 0, in favor of Sewanee, the championship of the south going to the winner.

Back at home on the mountain, its remarkable season over, the Sewanee squad was honored at an event the *Purple* captioned "The Football Supper" and described thusly:

"The varsity, with subs, and a few others who were fortunate enough to be involved, gathered at the house of the Vice-Chancellor (and Greek scholar Benjamin Lawton Wiggins) on Tuesday evening, December 5th, and partook of a delightful dinner given in honor of the team.

"Everything from soup to filberts, that could tempt the appetite of these delicate youths, was offered them, and one would have thought that the rigorous training-table had made their appetites as lusty as practice has their frames.

"After the nuts had been placed upon the table, Mr. Wiggins presided as toastmaster, and called upon Coach Suter, Mr. Lea, and Captain Seibels, in turn, to respond. The team then took matters in their own hands, and elected various members by acclamation to speak. 'Bud' delivered a eulogy on 'The Ladies.'

"After the dinner, Mrs. Wiggins received the team in the drawing room, assisted by the young ladies of the mountain. When an ice had been served, the company adjourned to the open air, and enjoyed a miniature pyrotechnic display, accompanied by 'Pap's' sonorous notes in 'That Good, Old-Time Religion.'

"For the benefit of those who have never been entertained at Fulford Hall, we may say that everyone enjoyed the evening heartily."

XV

The rest of their story

Sewanee was no one-year wonder. After the Iron Men took the school to the top of the football world in 1899, it continued as a power for more than a quarter-century before larger institutions with much more manpower brought change.

With nine of the '99 starters returning - only Keyes and Sims departed - and bolstered by several talented new-comers, the Tigers (as they would become known) posted a 6-1-1 record in 1900. Resuming the rivalry with Vanderbilt, they won that key game 11-10, played a scoreless tie with North Carolina and lost the season finale to Virginia 17-5 at Richmond. In addition to Vanderbilt, they defeated Bethel, Cumberland, Georgia, Georgia Tech and the University of Nashville.

Seibels, Simkins and Poole were named to *Outing* magazine's 1899 All-Southern team.

Sewanee won four Southern championships in the first decade of the 20th century, ultimately saw three players inducted into the College Football Hall of Fame and posted impressive records against such name schools as Alabama, Auburn, Georgia Tech, Tennessee, Louisiana State and Mississippi.

The Hall of Fame inductees are Henry D. Phillips, 1901-04 lineman; Frank A. Juhan, 1908-10 center, and Diddy Seibels, 1896-1900 halfback.

All told, Sewanee has had four undefeated seasons and 12 seasons with only one defeat.

A charter member of the Southeastern Conference founded in 1933, Sewanee by then was outmanned by much larger schools with greater resources. After losing 44 consecutive SEC games, the school withdrew from the SEC in 1940 and announced that henceforth it would play only other non-scholarship teams. Vice-chancellor Alexander Guerry had made withdrawal from bigtime football a condition of his taking the university reins.

Today Sewanee competes in the Southern Collegiate Athletic Conference against such other nonsubsidized teams as Washington & Lee, Rhodes College of Memphis and Millsaps of Jackson, Miss. Crowds ranging from 1,000 to 2,000 of students, alumni and townspeople gather at McGee (formerly Hardee) Field and watch their student athletes perform on the turf where Diddy Seibels, Ormond Simkins and their '99 teammates practiced for their once-in-a-lifetime trip.

An occasional football program note recalls the Iron Men. And a simple plaque, one of several at the base of a football-field flagpole, notes the five road victories in six days. But modern Sewanee coaches do not cite the Iron Men to inspire their non-scholarship teams.

Will Meadows, Jr., a standout Purple back in the 1980s and later a medical student at the University of South Alabama, recalled that his coaches referred occasionally to Sewanee football tradition but did not single out the Iron Men. Except for a fun poster with the caption "And on the seventh day they rested" and the flagpole plaque, there were no public reminders of the 1899 team.

Meadows, who had played high school ball for Birmingham-area Vestavia, said he had wondered during his high school football what playing before huge college crowds would be like, but when decision time came, he chose Sewanee and its quality education. As for the challenge of playing non-scholarship football on the mountain, he said, "You have to love to play. Hitting on practice days can't be as all-out as at other schools, but the hitting on game day is no different" from large-school games.

Because of Sewanee's high academic requirements, Meadows knew he would be prepared to be choosey about a profession. "You get an education (at Sewanee) that lets you go as far as ability permits," he said.

Football historians today recognize the Iron Men and their feat of winning five road games in six days without giving up a point. Occasionally a sports columnist searching for a topic on a slow day reaches into his files, takes out the Sewanee clips and retells the Iron Men story for a new generation of readers. On family bookshelves and in attic trunks, faded newspaper clippings preserve the story.

The *Sports Illustrated* issue of Oct. 16, 1961, described the memorable trip in an article entitled "The Miracle of Sewanee." In 1989 *New York Newsday* retold the story beneath the headline "5 football wins in 6 days." *Nashville Banner* executive and longtime sports editor Fred Russell, Vanderbilt graduate and close observer of the Sewanee scene, has reminisced in his column about the trip, as have numerous other sports reporters such as Alf Van Hoose and Clyde Bolton of the *Birmingham News*, the late syndicated columnist Grantland Rice and Herman Helms of the *Charlotte Observer*.

Among the many books that have devoted a chapter or thereabout to the '99 Sewanee season are Fuzzy Woodruff's *History of Southern Football*, Zipp Newman's *The Impact of Southern Football*, Tom Perrin's *Football: A College History* and Clyde Bolton's *Unforgettable Days in Southern Football*.

The late James Gregg, Sewanee alumnus and sports staffer for the *New York Daily News*, provided a detailed history of Sewanee teams in his *Sports History of the University of the South, 1875-1948*.

And *The NCAA News* made the Sewanee story a permanent part of its records with an article in November 1983: "1899 'ironman' team at Sewanee remains unequalled for endurance."

And what became of the hardy band of 24—coach, manager, trainer and 21 players—who left the mountain campus to do what seemed the impossible?

With the assistance of Sewanee historiographer Arthur Ben Chitty, his wife Elizabeth N. Chitty, and archivist Anne Armour, this researcher put together a followup file. Even as this text headed for publication, letters and phone calls pursued the Iron Men among descendants, newspapers and libraries.

COACH BILLY SUTER remained at Sewanee two more seasons, his 1900 and 1901 teams winning 10 games, losing three and tieing two. He moved on to Georgetown where he coached five years, worked with the U.S. Forestry Service for a time, became publisher of the *Nashville Tennessean*, where he renewed ties with *Tennessean* founder Luke Lea, 1899 football manager, then continued active in the newspaper publishing field at the *Washington Herald* and *Philadelphia Evening Star.* He became known as a "doctor of sick newspapers." Suter died Oct. 31, 1946.

MANAGER LUKE LEA, who is generally credited with putting together the Iron Men schedule, earned a master's degree at Sewanee, then a law degree at Columbia, taught at Sewanee and entered politics. He founded the *Nashville Tennessean*, became at 32 the youngest-ever U.S. senator and the last chosen by the Tennessee Legislature.

Lea was an Army artillery colonel in World War I, staying true to his adventurous lifestyle in an almost-successful attempt to kidnap the exiled German kaiser after hostilities ended.

He built a political and financial empire in Tennessee, served part of a prison sentence in connection with the failure of a North Carolina bank, and was pardoned by Tennessee. He died in Nashville Nov. 18, 1945.

TRAINER CAL BURROWS. Sewanee sources believe the popular black "rubdown man" on the Iron Men trip was a trash and garbage collector in the mountain community.

Quarterback WILLIAM BLACKBURN "WARBLER" WILSON captained the 1900 Sewanee team. He helped keep the Purple team unbeaten until the season finale against Virginia. Having earned a law degree, he went back to Rock Hill, S.C., to practice. He served for a time as county attorney and was elected to the Legislature. Wilson made a name for himself at Sewanee and passed that name to descendants—at last check to William Blackburn "Blackie" Wilson VI!

In an interview with the *Charlotte Observer*'s Herman Helms, the 1899 and 1900 Sewanee Iron Man declined a suggestion that he considered modern football players "softies," but he told Helms they give him the heebegeebies "going into those confound huddles all the time." Wilson died Dec. 8, 1958.

Left halfback RINGLAND FISHER "REX" KILPATRICK returned for the 1900 season, worked toward a law degree and became a builder and investment banker in the New York area. Among structures he built was the city's Fox Film Building.

Active in the New York Athletic Club, Kilpatrick renewed acquaintance there with ex-Auburn coach John Heisman. A brother, John Reed Kilpatrick, who had starred in Yale football, was for a time chairman of Madison Square Garden. Rex died in Spring Lake, N.J., in November 1955.

Right halfback HENRY G. "DIDDY" SEIBELS completed his BA degree in the summer of 1900 and played on the successful 1900 team, captained by "Warbler" Wilson. Although he studied law, Seibels did not earn a law degree. He served a short while as headmaster of Sewanee Grammar School, then moved to Birmingham to manage the insurance department of a business headed by Sewanee schoolmate Robert S. Jemison, Jr. Seibels later founded his own insurance company and was a successful Birmingham business leader more than half a century.

A talented and competitive golfer, Seibels won the Alabama state championship in 1922 and once lost a tournament match to golfing great Bobby Jones. In 1955 Sewanee conferred an honorary degree of civil law on Seibels.

One of the last surviving members of the Iron Men team, Seibels died in 1967 at age 91.

He was inducted into the College Football Hall of Fame in 1973 and into the Alabama Sports Hall of Fame in 1992.

Fullback ORMOND SIMKINS, describd by Coach Suter in a 1944 interview with Grantland Rice as "one of the greatest players I ever saw," returned for the 1900 season and was class valedictorian. He followed his father into law practice in Texas, then for a time was master of West

Texas Military Academy in San Antonio. He practiced law in Dallas and later worked for the War Risk Bureau in Washington.

Simkins had suffered injuries to both legs while playing football and at some point in later years one leg was amputated. While working in Washington, he entered Georgetown Hospital and died Dec. 4, 1921 while undergoing amputation of the other leg. He was 42.

An editor friend at the *Dallas Times-Herald* wrote of Simkins: "He combined a charming modesty with achievement....He got results and then tried to show that the results belonged to somebody else." Perhaps teammate Diddy Seibels was thinking of that quality when he told his sons that Simkins was the Iron Men's best player.

A field house named for Simkins is incorporated into Sewanee's Juhan Gym.

End BARTLET ET ULTIMUS SIMS earned a medical degree at Tulane, served in the medical corps in World War I and was a physician/surgeon in Bryan, Texas. He was killed in an automobile accident in Texas in January 1934.

End HUGH MILLER THOMPSON "BUNNY" PEARCE returned for the 1900 season, studied theology and was commandant of Sewanee Grammar School. He was a Navy chaplain in World War I. He died Nov. 24, 1935, in Pensacola, Fla.

Tackle JOHN WILLIAM JONES was a football returnee in 1900. He became an Episcopal clergyman serving in Texas, California, Iowa, Illinois and Kansas. His competing-careers marriage (Mrs. Jones was an actress) became increasingly strained, and on Oct. 8, 1923, in Kansas City he took his own life. *The New York Times* reported that a letter to his wife referred to the couple's concern for but unsuccessful efforts to provide a suitable home for their five children.

A short time before his death, Jones had resigned as archdeacon for western Kansas.

Tackle RICHARD ELLIOTT BOLLING earned an MD

degree and went to Redlands, Calif. to practice. He was there until 1910, then his trail vanished.

Guard HENRY SHERIDAN KEYES earned pharmaceutical and medical degrees and served in the U.S. medical corps. In later life he became a religious zealot, predicting the end of the world. He died in 1955.

Guard WILLIAM STIRLING CLAIBORNE returned to play on the 1900 team, continued theology study and became known as the "apostle to the mountain folk" for his work among Tennessee mountain people. The story is told that once, when a rowdy youth was trying to interrupt a Claiborne sermon, the powerfully built former guard continued holding an open Bible in one hand and with the other picked up the rowdy and set him outside the door, never interrupting his sermon.

Claiborne founded the St. Andrew's School for Mountain Boys, refounded St. Mary's School, and established Emerald-Hodgson Hospital, all at Sewanee, wrote a book entitled *Boy in the Mountains*, and became archdeacon of Tennessee. He died in 1933.

Center WILLIAM HENRY POOLE played football in 1900, completed a theology degree at the Episcopal Theological School in Cambridge, Mass., and served in Maryland, Ohio, Michigan and Virginia. Poole worked for the UMCA in France in 1918. He died in Graham, Va., June 12, 1921.

Substitutes

RALPH PETERS BLACK became a first-string end on the 1900 team. After earning a B.A. degree, he did graduate work at Columbia University and was an engineer with the Pennsylvania Railroad. In World War I he was a first lieutenant (later a major) with the 32nd Engineers AEF. He taught civil engineering at Sewanee, then at Georgia Tech for many years. The professor was known to his students as "Rip" and "the Major." He bequeathed funds for a golf clubhouse at Sewanee and gave the Hardee (now McGee) Field flagpole, which bears plaques to outstanding Sewanee teams. In an interview with an Atlanta sports writer, Black said the modern free-substitution rule killed the spirit of teamwork and made for sissies. He died in Atlanta in January 1960.

HARRIS GOODWIN COPE, who had playing time as a freshman on the 1899 team, went on to play in 1900 and was captain of the 1901 team. He served as Sewanee coach from 1908 till 1916. His 1909 Sewanee team defeated arch-rival Vanderbilt 16-5. After coaching days at Sewanee, Cope entered business for a time but suffered setbacks and in 1922 returned to coaching ranks, this time at Howard College in Birmingham. After two years at Howard he died just before the 1924 season began.

PRESTON SMITH BROOKS, JR., although not earning a degree, became a successful merchant, with his brother operating the P.S. Brooks Store in Sewanee. He died in Sewanee Feb. 3, 1950.

DANIEL BALDWIN HULL played on the 1900 team and returned to his hometown of Savannah, Ga., where he became a boxing promoter. A young son was struck and killed by a drunken driver, and Hull was despondent for years over the loss. He died in September 1967.

JOSEPH LEE KIRBY-SMITH earned an M.D. degree in 1906 and served in the Public Health Service during World War I. He taught dermatology at New York University and practiced in Jacksonville, Fla. He died there Nov. 5, 1939.

CHARLES QUINTARD GRAY, who had been a substitute for Rex Kilpatrick after starting a game at left halfback, earned a degree and entered the life insurance business in Florida and later was an insurance broker in Dallas. He died in Dallas Jan. 11, 1906.

LANDON RANDOLPH MASON earned a medical degree in January 1902 but lived only a few months after that. He contracted typhoid fever and died in Marshall, Va., April 13 that same year.

FLOY HOFFMAN PARKER played football again in 1900 and entered banking and politics in Louisiana and Mississippi, serving in the Mississippi Legislature. He was president of the Bank of Canton, then president of Deposit Guaranty & Trust Co. in Jackson. He died in Canton on April 18, 1954.

ALBERT TREAT DAVIDSON returned to play football in 1900. After graduation he was employed at the Augusta (Ga.) Arsenal. He died in Augusta March 14, 1946.

ANDREW CLEVELAND EVINS worked in Atlanta and died in Spartanburg, S.C., about 1917.

XVI

So, what place for Sewanee '99?

Almost a century after Sewanee's Iron Men feat, football historians still haven't agreed on an appropriate trophy case for the five road triumphs in six days.

Was the Texas trip—on which the Purple shut out Texas, Texas A&M, Tulane, LSU and Ole Miss—a fluke, a chance roll of the dice by an adventurous manager and a willing-to-go-along coach?

Or was it a well-thought-out schedule arranged by a brainy manager who knew precisely what he was doing, played through by a squad blessed with talent and experience, and a young coach who perhaps saw the trip as a short-cut to national prominence and promotion to a larger-school coaching job?

The latter seems far more likely. Luke Lea's negotiating genius quickly surfaced in politics and business after he left Sewanee. Billy Suter's football-coaching star never again soared so high after the glittering '99 season, but he, too, succeeded in other fields.

So what place in history for Sewanee '99, its five road shutouts in six days, its unbeaten, untied and almost-unscored-on season of 12 wins? Ten of the 12 victories were against Southern Intercollegiate Athletic Association opponents, putting Sewanee in the record books for most conference games played and most won in a season. And, because of the agreed-on "championship challenge," a case can be made for calling the Sewanee-North Carolina contest America's first "bowl" game, despite its having been on the schedule all season.

College football has had other remarkable teams with remarkable seasons. One such team was Duke in 1938. Coached by Wallace Wade, Duke rolled through the season without a loss, tie, or opposing point. Only in the last minute of the post-season Rose Bowl against Southern Cal were the Blue Devils done in, and then on a touchdown pass Wade insisted was illegal. Nevertheless, the record book shows Southern Cal 7, Duke 3.

Other schools could point to "greatest seasons." Sewanee '99 has company and to spare.

Not so, the five wins in six days. That feat stands alone, majestic and unmatched. There was nothing like it before, there's been nothing like it since and today's once-a-week schedules all but guarantee the Sewanee feat needs no asterisk in the record book.

So the question persists: What place for Sewanee '99?

Perhaps a special category called "Iron Men in Sports" should be created. Grantland Rice made a motion in that direction in his book *The Tumult and the Shouting*, published in 1954. Rice, in his time dean of sportswriters, listed these iron-man nominees:

—Ty Cobb, who "traveled at top speed on a pair of fairly thin legs for 24 years....He played in more than 3,000 ball games and scored over 4,000 runs."

—Bob Fitzsimmons, "who was fighting bouts at 18 and didn't stop until he was 52...and won the world's heavyweight title from James J. Corbett...when he was 35!"

—Lou Gehrig..."who finally retired after eight games in 1939 because of the sudden and slashing destruction to his body" after he "played 2,130 consecutive games over a period of 15 years without missing his appointment at first base!" Amyotrophic lateral sclerosis was wasting his body away.

Rice was attending Vanderbilt University while Billy Suter was coaching at Sewanee. Almost half a century later, in 1944, he interviewed Suter about the '99 football team and wrote a column on him and his Sewanee team, yet did not mention the five-games-in-six-days trip in a chapter on the iron men of sports. Apparently he was focusing on *individual* "iron men" and had no intention of naming iron-man *teams*. Even so, it is odd that he did not even tip his hat toward Sewanee while nominating his iron men of sports.

On a slow night at the nearest pub, the question may come up: "How would the 1899 Sewanee team stack up against modern powers like Florida State, Miami, Alabama, Auburn, Tennessee and Texas?" If the question is asked, the pub's football court should rule it unanswerable for lack of common denominators. As the *Birmingham News'* Clyde Bolton wrote in his *Unforgettable Days in Southern Football,* even to attempt a comparison would be ludicrous.

Sewanee '99 then must stand on its own *feat,* in its own time.

Perhaps the views of a highly successful modern-day coach and an All-America lineman who played both offense and defense could put the Sewanee feat in focus.

Florida State's Bobby Bowden, whose teams make college football's Top Ten year after year, had this comment:

"In 1981 my football team, Florida State, played Nebraska, Pittsburgh, Ohio State, Notre Dame and LSU on successive weekends, away. (Editor's note: And won three of the five.) This was a modern-day freak in scheduling. Now, if this catches your attention, what do you think about Sewanee playing Texas, Texas A&M, Tulane, LSU and Mississippi within a six-day period, away from home? It is unparalleled in football history."

Fred Sington, All-America tackle at Alabama in 1930, knew first-hand from many bruising Saturday afternoons, what it meant to stay on the field all 60 minutes. "Just to play both ways was a full deal," he said. "It was an honor; you never wanted to come out of a game. To play five games in six days, all on the road, was an awesome feat, an example of tremendous physical stamina."

Perhaps then Sewanee deserves football's all-time trophy for stamina and endurance. In which case, consider the trophy awarded—and retired.